T0207916

15 Things

You Should Know

Wisdom for Life's Journey

John Carroll

authorHOUSE®

AuthorHouse™
1663 Liberty Drive
Bloomington, IN 47403
www.authorhouse.com
Phone: 1 (800) 839-8640

© 2018 John Carroll. All rights reserved.

No part of this book may be reproduced, stored in a retrieval system, or transmitted by any means without the written permission of the author.

Published by AuthorHouse 10/15/2018

ISBN: 978-1-5462-6431-6 (sc)
ISBN: 978-1-5462-6430-9 (e)

Library of Congress Control Number: 2018912327

Print information available on the last page.

Any people depicted in stock imagery provided by Getty Images are models, and such images are being used for illustrative purposes only.
Certain stock imagery © Getty Images.

This book is printed on acid-free paper.

Because of the dynamic nature of the Internet, any web addresses or links contained in this book may have changed since publication and may no longer be valid. The views expressed in this work are solely those of the author and do not necessarily reflect the views of the publisher, and the publisher hereby disclaims any responsibility for them.

CONTENTS

SPECIAL DEDICATION

This book is dedicated to Laura, my beautiful and courageous wife, who lost her final battle with metastatic breast cancer on March 4, 2016. Throughout our lives together, you were the source of my strength, my inspiration, and my why.

You brought so much love, life, laughter, and beauty into my world. By doing so, you helped me in so many ways to grow as a person and to become a better husband, father, friend, and leader.

Lollie, you are the love of my life, my forever one, and I will always love you. Thank you for blessing me with your unconditional love, encouragement and support, and for a lifetime of wonderful memories and happiness.

ACKNOWLEDGMENTS

Getting back to writing once again has been a difficult challenge for me since my wife's passing. It has been hard to find my mojo without Laura here every step of the way to offer her loving input, encouragement, and guidance.

However, I'm blessed to have the love and support of my three children, Melanie, Daniel, and Brent, and great clients and friends who have helped me through the creative process to complete the book. Thank for being there for me when I needed it most.

Special acknowledgments for good friends Sandy Anderson and Rhonda Hailey. It was your positive feedback on a blog article I wrote several years ago that provided the impetus for this book. Thank you for the encouragement and support. Your friendship has been a blessing to me.

To my Lord and Savior, Jesus Christ, thank you for your divine guidance and strength. The words "don't overthink it, just live" still ring in my ears as an affirmation of my belief that all things are possible through you.

To the AuthorHouse Publishing team of Karen Stapleton, Rhea Nolan, Joy M and Jose Ortega. Thank you so much for all of the support you have provided throughout the process to help me get the book out of my head and out the door.

I so appreciate each of your contributions.

INTRODUCTION

15 Things You Should *Know: Wisdom for Life's Journey* is all about life, or more appropriately, it is a reflection of life's journey.

As you will discover, the book is loaded with great quotes, fun facts, tips, life lessons, and relevant content for the ages. All designed to make you pause, laugh, think, question, and thoughtfully consider where you are today in your journey and the opportunities and challenges that are ahead.

You'll also find a few I-had-no-idea and what-the-heck moments, as well as lots of random thoughts thrown in for good measure just to hold your attention and keep things interesting.

Each chapter is a collection of my own home remedies, suggested actions, and answers to things you need to know that apply in business and to all other areas of life as well. This is a compilation derived from my personal life experiences, more than 175 articles I have written over the years, and research conducted on the selected chapter topics.

From the "The Journey" to "The End?," *15 Things You* Should *Know: Wisdom for Life's Journey* will educate, encourage, challenge, and inspire you to continue to change, grow, and accomplish great things throughout your lifetime. Most importantly, it will challenge you to make a positive difference in the lives of others.

We will all reach the finish line someday—this fact is undeniable. Whether you are walking or running to reach the final destination doesn't matter. It won't matter what obstacles you had to overcome or how many steps it took to get there. What will matter is the difference you made in the lives of the people you met along the way.

Stay positive about your life, the possibilities for a bright future, and the road ahead. If you are struggling today in any of the areas outlined in the book's chapters, I sincerely hope you'll find some great takeaways to help you overcome these challenges from the pages to follow.

There are no guarantees in life—only opportunities. Starting is the initial step or action that will ultimately lead to achievement and success in any endeavor. With this in mind, let's get started …

CHAPTER 1

The Journey

It's a marathon, not a sprint.

Why are we always in such a hurry, rushing from place to place and from one task to the next? Life is not a race; it is a journey. Much like fine wine, it's to be savored and enjoyed, not rushed through or brushed aside like the passage of the wind.

If you were told that today was your last day on earth, would you be in such a hurry to reach the finish line? Probably not. So what's the rush?

There are 86,400 seconds in each day. How will you spend them to get the most out of today? Now, let me clarify: Getting the most out of each day is not about quantity. It is about quality. However, most of us are guilty of trying to stuff one hundred pounds of poop into a fifty-pound bag each day and then wondering why we are so stressed out and our lives are in such a state of disarray.

We get the most out of each day—and the journey as a whole—when we feed our souls and serve others. However, many people are so busy being busy that they miss out on the sheer joy of living. As George Leonard points out in his book *Mastery: The Keys to Success and Long-Term Fulfillment*, "The real juice of life, whether it be sweet or bitter, is to be found not nearly so much in the products of our efforts as in the process of living itself, in how it feels to be alive."

I don't think God will grant us an extra pair of wings (if we are fortunate enough to get into heaven) for completing more projects or items on our to-do lists than the next person during our time here on earth. So why are we compelled to rush though each day and fill up the white space on our daily calendars with endless activities, appointments, meetings, and conference calls in order to validate our self-worth?

From the very moment of birth, our lives' journeys begins to move us toward an inevitable conclusion. It's part of the circle of life, and each of us has an expiration date. We are born and we die, but everything in between—the journey—is where life truly happens. Each day we are given is a blessing to be celebrated. Don't waste the time you've been given because life changes with each step we take.

Worldwide, in 2015, the average life expectancy at birth was seventy and a half years (sixty-eight years and four months for males and seventy-two years and eight months for females), according to the United Nations World Population Prospects 2015 Revision. If you are blessed to live a long life, it's a marathon, not a sprint, so pace yourself. Take a time-out and think about how good it feels to just be alive.

Fun fact: If you walk ten thousand steps a day (roughly 4.25 miles), you will travel more than 1,500 miles in a year. Think of how much you'll experience and how much your life will change along the way by embarking on this part of your journey.

There are no guarantees on the journey, only opportunities. The most extraordinary thing is that our lives can be forever changed in the blink of an eye by a single event or a single step. Your life's journey, the sweet and the bitter, will encompass a series of defining moments that occur continuously throughout your lifetime. These defining moments and life-changing experiences are the guiding forces that shape our lives and help us remember who we are, where we've been, and where we hope to go in the future.

Sometimes life is about the ability to believe in where you are going even when you're not sure what lies ahead.

— Unknown

Each person's journey is different and unique. However, each of us will face many common life-changing experiences: a high school and maybe college graduation; the birth of a child; the death of a loved one; a major accident, illness, or injury; the purchase of a new home; the loss of a job or career change; a move to a new city, state, or country; and the list goes on and on.

The journey is *your* life, and no one can make it for you. But that doesn't mean you should not invite others along for the ride. Family, friends, neighbors, coworkers, and others will all play important roles in your journey. And as you will discover, many of those who join in your travels will not be there at the end.

Much as on a bus ride, people will hop on and hop off at various points along the way, each one leaving you with something, whether it be a blessing or a lesson that you can build upon to ultimately become the best version of yourself. And if you are fortunate, it will be a long, joyous ride filled with many great people, memories, and surprises.

What are you feeding your soul?

Many people struggle daily trying to come to grips with the meaning of life rather than just enjoying the journey. They agonize over questions for which there are no answers, at least not in this life. *Who am I? Why am I here? What's next?* Rather than wasting time seeking answers to the unanswerable, do this instead: Don't overthink it. Just live. Just live your life in the moment.

Fun fact: Twelve minutes of daily prayer over an eight-week period can change the brain to such an extent that the change can be measured in a brain scan.

I encourage you to unplug and set aside time for yourself every day for prayer, reading, meditation and reflection, and exercise. Make time for those important things that will help restore and reinvigorate your body, mind, and spirit. Inhale the positive, exhale the negative, and set your intentions for what you want to accomplish that day.

What are you grateful for today?

Are you grateful for a loving family, good health, a new home, a great career, a planned vacation trip, your faith? The list can go on and on from here. Researchers are discovering that gratitude doesn't just make you feel like a better person; it is actually good for your health. So take time to give thanks to start your day.

"Clinical trials indicate that the practice of gratitude can have dramatic and lasting effects on a person's life," according to Robert A. Emmons, professor of psychology at UC Davis. "It can lower your blood pressure, improve immune function, and facilitate more efficient sleep." In addition, it can also improve heart health.

There are so many things we overlook in the hustle and bustle of daily life that we should be thankful for. Take time out to identify what you are most grateful for each day and declare it!

How are you serving others?

But don't stop there—share it with others. One of the best ways that I know to show the power of gratitude is by dedicating your time, talents, and treasures in service to others. Don't just be grateful. Give back. Show people that you care by sharing your knowledge and resources. Be a mentor. You may never know how a kind word, thoughtful advice, or a random act of kindness on your part could change someone's life forever.

Pay it forward. The next time you're not feeling that attitude of gratitude for all your blessings, consider this: 80 percent of the world's population lives on less than $10 a day. More than three billion people globally live on less than $2.50 per day. Your life's journey could be much worse, and these statistics help to put things in the proper perspective.

Take the time to demonstrate your gratitude through caregiving and stewardship in your business, local community, church, outreach programs, or charitable organizations. As my good friend Alisa Bell points out in her book, *50 Golden Nuggets: Laser Sharp Quotes Designed to Shape Your Day,* "Growth is a journey in which we must actively participate." The same can be said of our lives as a whole.

Each of us *will* change, grow, and accomplish great things during our lifetimes. This I know to be true, whether you are young, old, or somewhere in between. My advice to help you on the journey is don't just be. *Be great*!

- **B**elieve in yourself.
- **E**njoy *your* life.
- **G**ive generously to those in need.
- **R**espect all living things.
- **E**nergize and excite others.
- **A**void energy vampires.
- **T**ransform your thoughts into actions.

We will *all* reach the finish line someday; this fact is undeniable. Whether you walk or run to reach the final destination doesn't matter. It won't matter what obstacles you will have to overcome or how many steps it takes to get there. What will matter is the difference you make in the lives of the people you meet along the way.

So buy the ticket, take the ride, enjoy the journey!

CHAPTER 2

Achievement

You can't expect to win if you don't compete.

I know this quote sounds like a blinding flash of the obvious (BFO) when it rolls off the tip of your tongue—but not so much in today's world. Things have tilted so far from center that many people confuse starting something new or just showing up with winning or achievement. They're not the same.

To be clear, achievement, by definition, is a thing done successfully, typically by effort, courage, or skill. The process or fact of achieving something. For example, getting out of bed is *not* an achievement, although it may feel like it on a Monday morning after a big weekend of partying. Why? It requires little effort, courage, or skill. You get the point.

Zig Ziglar had a term for this failure to start: "Getting cooked in the squat." Ziglar shared a wonderful story from his youth in several of his inspirational videos to illustrate what it meant to get cooked in the squat. He also pointed out that "you don't have to be great to start, but you have to start to be great." *Starting is the initial step or* action *that ultimately leads to achievement.*

> *Action may not always bring happiness, but there is no happiness without action.*
>
> — Benjamin Disraeli

All of us have that friend or relative who we can relate to in this illustration. They talk a lot about their goals and dreams, but these never seem to get off the ground. And there are always a litany of reasons why. I refer to them as the one-of-these-days people. My parents were one-of-these-days people. They always talked about having a better life, car, house, vacation trip, etc. But none of their dreams ever materialized.

Why the reluctance or failure to launch?

The term *failure to launch* is an increasingly popular way to describe the difficulties some young adults face when transitioning into the next phase of development—a stage that involves greater independence and responsibility. However, a failure to launch covers a much broader spectrum than a young adult's reluctance to leave the nest.

Most often when we fail to achieve our personal goals, it can be attributed to one or more of the following reasons:

- excuses
- fear of success

- lack of planning
- not setting priorities and deadlines
- giving up when it gets too tough

However, none of the above is the primary reason most people fail to reach their goals. (See the number-one reason in the paragraphs that follow.)

Let's face it: nobody intentionally sets out to fail. However, oftentimes we undermine our own success due to a lack of effort and action. In business, failure is most commonly tied to a lack of time, people, capital, resources, or sales. But it can also be the result of poor planning, execution, accountability, and leadership. Speaking of accountability and leadership …

Fun fact: Ninety-seven percent of the people who *quit* too soon, or never get started, are employed by the 3 percent who never gave up.

The most powerful leadership tool available to you in achieving success at anything is your own personal example. Leadership is also where accountability begins and ends. Have you ever stopped to think about why the word *accountability* carries such a negative connotation in our modern society? Even the very definition of accountability is punitive and makes it sound like one of those bad four-letter words we were told not to say when we were children.

When we think of accountability, we think about who's responsible, and we think about blame. The main difference between *responsibility* and *accountability* is that responsibility can be shared, while accountability cannot. Being accountable not only means being *responsible* for something but also being answerable for *your actions*. If you have no desire for a better life or self-improvement, then accountability is irrelevant.

Now (drumroll please), the *number-one reason people fail to reach their goals* is that there are no real consequences for their inaction. If there is no penalty for a lack of action on my part, what is my motivation? Answer: If you accept the status quo, then there is no motivation. However, if you are willing to tolerate mediocrity in yourself and others, then don't expect great results or a meaningful life. Real life just doesn't work that way.

You playing small does not serve the world.

—Nelson Mandela

However, if you want to improve your lot in life, then it requires real action on your part. It requires you to be *accountable*; to engage and get started; to change, grow, and develop; and yes, to achieve something!

Achievement is synonymous with success. "People are as successful as they choose to be" is a quote we see quite often these days. It infers that success (or achievement) is a choice. What many people fail to recognize is that lack of action or a failure to start is also a choice—a choice that limits not only our success but our freedom as well.

Why? Because a lack of action will result in giving up control of our life choices to others. When we control the decisions, we can control the actions and the outcome. However, if we abdicate responsibility for our lives to others, they are no longer our lives. Now is that how you choose to live?

Here are some thoughts to consider to help you get started, take more control, and achieve greater success in your business and personal life.

1. Set reasonable goals for what you want to accomplish.
2. Be clear on how you define success.
3. Understand why the goal, project, etc. is important.
4. Hold yourself accountable for results.
5. Measure and track your performance.
6. Make course corrections where needed.
7. Celebrate your successes and keep going.

Where you are today is not your final destination. Many people fail to start because they become overwhelmed with how far they must go to reach the finish line. Don't focus on the distance you have to travel, but instead focus on the progress to be made today, next week, next month, etc. If you're serious about getting the most out of each day in your business and personal life, then stop thinking so much and make it happen.

Fear, procrastination, creative avoidance, laziness, apathy, boredom, etc. are all things that can keep us from getting started, competing, and achieving success. Plain and simple, you can't win in sports, business, or life if you don't compete on some level. More often than not, we are competing with ourselves in order to reach the intended target. However, there are a lot of folks out there today who believe we should get an award just for showing up.

I am not a big fan of participation trophies. The notion that everyone receives a trophy has taken the place of only rewarding those who achieve excellence in a specified activity. This is stinking thinking in my opinion and leads to a false sense of entitlement. Nothing gets done if all we do is occupy space. Achievement and a sense of accomplishment come not from just showing up but rather from doing your best and achieving a certain level of excellence.

What should we consider to be noteworthy achievements?

We often recognize and reward people for achieving specific milestones viewed as significant—for example, graduation from high school or college, receiving a promotion, or winning a sporting event. But what else should we consider to be achievements that did not make this list? Being a good husband or wife, a good mother or father, or a good neighbor or loyal friend?

How about giving birth or taking your first steps as a child, learning to play an instrument, writing a book, completing your first DIY home project, or mentoring a new business owner or a struggling friend? This list could go on forever. Should these important milestones not be considered noteworthy achievements? Or should success be limited to just winning trophies, awards, and plaques? The short answer is: no, success should not be just about winning awards.

When it comes to recognition, trophies, and awards remember this: Today's golden idol is tomorrow's brass commode. It doesn't take much to fall from grace, and then all of those trophies and accolades are swept aside and forgotten. Achievement is so much more than just competing and winning. Moreover, it should also be about continuous growth and development, self-discovery, and getting the most out of the journey, as I highlighted in chapter 1.

I was fortunate to have an outstanding career and received numerous awards, mementos, and accolades over the years. And trust me—I relished every single moment I was in the spotlight. However, I rarely think about those milestones and accomplishments today. In fact, you will see very little reflection of my college degrees, performance awards, plaques, trophies, etc. in my home. They are tucked away in boxes somewhere in the attic.

As I get older and further away from the glory days of my thirty-year corporate career, my definition of achievement has changed significantly, as have my priorities. Maybe some of you have experienced this same transformation. Today, I'm focused on the things I can do to be a better person while serving others and making a positive impact, rather than personal recognition and awards.

Being the best version of yourself, serving others, and making a difference—those are truly outstanding *achievements* I think we can all get behind.

CHAPTER 3

Relationships

If you fail to build relationships, you will.

Fail, that is. Relationships are a fundamental part of daily living. No matter what you want to achieve in this life, it is much easier if you have other people who can help and support you in the journey. So, let's all agree that success is impossible without building great relationships in every aspect of our lives.

Why are relationships so important?

Well first of all, they fulfill our most important basic need: love. We all need to love and to be loved. There is no other way to love and be loved than through relationships. What is the most important love relationship you will have in your lifetime?

Next to our relationship with God, if you are a believer, it is our relationship with self. The relationship we have with ourselves is the cornerstone for everything. It would be hard, if not impossible, to build great relationships with other people if we have a poor or unhealthy relationship with ourselves. Think about it.

The only person who will be with you for your entire life span, from beginning to end, is you. So first things first, you need to love yourself and develop a healthy self-image. To accomplish this, you must draw in the positive and filter out the negative self-talk, practice self-acceptance, and surround yourself with people who will love you, support you, and help you become the best version of yourself.

> *You are only one relationship away from changing your future.*
>
> —Chas Wilson

I absolutely love this quote, and it is so true! In the business world, your network is your net worth. On the flip side, you are also one relationship away from changing someone else's future. Let that sink in for a moment. I know the huge impact my first mentor had on my future. I highlighted the impact in our book, *Power of Inspiration: Dare to Be the Best YOU!,* and later in a blog article titled, "The Power of 14 Words."

Wilson's quote speaks to the powerful impact relationships, both good and bad, can have on the direction of our lives. Here's an example: During my sophomore year in college, I changed majors from accounting to marketing because of a negative relationship with a professor. I loved accounting but changed my life's direction because of this one bad experience. It worked out for the best in the end, but it still had a profound impact on my life choices at the time. Has this ever happened to you?

Now this certainly holds true in love relationships as well, where finding that special someone is a major (hopefully positive) future life-changing event for both parties.

Fun fact: Marriage is good for your heart. According to an article by Brittany Wong, "In one recent study out of New York University's Lagone Medical Center, researchers found that married men and women had a five percent lower chance of cardiovascular disease compared to single folks."

Beyond a *healthy* marital relationship, we will also enjoy numerous relationships in many other areas throughout our lives. Particularly in the business world, these relationships can be complicated, complex, multilayered, and, yes, adversarial. Why? Because we are dealing with feelings and emotions, interests, expectations, past experiences, personal biases, organizational politics, boundaries, and priorities that may or may not always be in alignment.

Whether in business or any other area, the goal should be to establish a win-win outcome where both parties feel good about the direction. This will help to ensure the viability and longevity of the relationship. From my forty-plus years in business, I have learned there is no secret potion, magic beans, or fairy dust required to develop a successful relationship.

What constitutes a successful relationship?

The short answer is: one that works well for both parties. It is much easier to achieve success when you are focused on the needs of others and are not overly invested in your own. Great relationships are more than something we desire; they are essential for a healthy, happy, well-balanced, and productive life. However, building a successful relationship doesn't happen overnight. Successful relationships are give and take. You must work at them, and they require time, patience, and commitment.

Fun fact: People you meet accidentally are more likely to become some of the most important individuals in your life.

Think about those great relationships you have enjoyed most in your life. What did they have in common? Of the many articles I have read on the topic of successful relationships, these are the common qualities that are most prevalent:

- honesty
- trust
- respect
- communication
- connection
- compromise
- shared values
- loyalty
- commitment

Every relationship is different. However, it would be very difficult to build a successful relationship without these qualities being present.

In addition, part of building healthy, successful relationships is removing toxic people from your life. What I've learned through my own interactions with others is not all relationships are equal. Human nature being what it is, some people bring more joy and others only problems. If you're a kind-hearted person, you may have a strong desire to treat every relationship the same.

However, in doing so, you will soon discover that toxic people take up more time, are more demanding, and, unfortunately, bring little or no value to the relationship. Don't be afraid to say goodbye to someone who is an energy vampire and a negative influence in your life. Removing toxic people will free up space so you can devote more time to cultivating those positive, long-lasting relationships that will enrich your life and, more importantly, enable you to enrich the lives of others.

Not only are relationships not equal but relationship priorities tend to shift during the various stages of life. For example, when we are small children, our most important relationships are with our parents and close family members. As we get a little older, our friends, classmates, teachers, teammates, coaches, etc. become the relationship priorities. And then as we grow into adulthood, our spouses, children, bosses, coworkers, and neighbors become our relationship priorities.

Why do relationships fail?

The number-one reason relationships fail is a lack of or breach of trust. Trust is the currency from which all relationships are built. Relationships can start to fall apart very quickly when it is apparent that the parties are only looking out for themselves and are not committed to making the relationship a priority. Once trust has been broken, it is highly unlikely the relationship will survive.

Some or all of the qualities I highlighted earlier that comprise a successful relationship are elements that may be missing in a failed one. In addition, here are some of the other common indicators to be aware of in a relationship going in the wrong direction.

- different expectations or priorities
- compatibility issues
- narcissism or selfishness
- growing in different directions
- financial challenges
- lack of support

Successful relationships don't just take care of themselves. They require proper care and feeding in order to grow and develop. If you see warning signs to indicate an important relationship is on the rocks, consider how to change course in order to improve it and increase the odds of its survival.

How can we improve our relationships with others?

First and foremost, be committed to the relationship and be present. This holds true for *all* relationships: family members, friends, coworkers, etc.

Second, show a genuine interest in the other person, and in enhancing the relationship, by providing helpful support when and where *the other person* requires it.

Third, bring something to the table—something of value to the other person. Also be sure you make the effort to give first in all of your interactions.

Fourth, be real, honest, and transparent in your dealings with others. No one wants to be lied to or feel like the other person is playing games or holding back.

Finally, always be kind, considerate, and generous. The Golden Rule will never go out of style, so treat people the way you want to be treated.

The most important things in life aren't things.

—Anthony J. D 'Angelo

In the end, *love* and *relationships* are all that really matter. As we approach the conclusion of life's journey, we won't be focused on awards and achievements. The size of our bank accounts, the size of our homes, or the kind of cars we drove will be of little importance. All of those things we accumulated throughout the course of our lives will no longer be of any significance.

What will matter is that we are surrounded by the people we care about most: our loved ones. And that we made a difference in the lives of others we touched through the valued relationships cultivated over a lifetime. Don't wait until those final moments to make this a priority.

Building those great, value-based relationships and changing lives should be a priority every day that you are above ground. So get started (if you have not already). You and the other important people in your life will be the better for it.

CHAPTER 4

Competence

Loving what you're doing is almost as important as knowing.

Competence is not a word that gets tossed around much these days. *Incompetent* seems to be used more often in our modern, negative society. But let's all agree upfront that one of the keys to success in anything is being good at what you do. This is where competence plays a distinct role.

By definition, competence is the ability to do something successfully or efficiently. When we think of competence, words like *ability*, *knowledge*, *skill*, *proficiency*, *expertise*, and *mastery* come to mind. Competence is also associated with accomplishment. We will talk more about accomplishment in chapter 5 when we address performance.

Fun fact: Incompetent people are often so incompetent that they don't even realize their own incompetence.

This phenomenon is commonly referred to as *unconscious incompetency*, a psychological state of awareness and learning. The four stages of competence, or learning, are a psychological model used in adaptive learning to assess skill gaps and help the student learner move from one stage to the next. These four stages include:

1. Unconscious incompetence
2. Conscious incompetence
3. Conscious competence
4. Unconscious competence

Understanding where students are in their knowledge of a particular topic will assist the trainer in identifying training needs and develop objectives to more effectively reach the target audience.

Okay, enough psychobabble. I just wanted to provide a very brief introduction to the topic of competence before we explore its importance in more direct terms.

> *I couldn't wait for success, so I went ahead without it.*
>
> —Jonathan Winters

Before a learning experience begins, we are unaware of what or how much we know (unconscious incompetence). By charging ahead, much like Jonathan Winters in the quote above, we run the risk of not reaching the level of proficiency required for success because the requisite knowledge, skills, or preparation is lacking. This ready, fire, aim mentality is far too common in the business world today and has resulted in numerous costly missteps and failed business ventures.

Fun fact: Ignorant people are more likely to believe they are brilliant, while competent people are more likely to underestimate themselves.

This is so true. Much of my corporate leadership experience was in startup or turnaround assignments within large corporations. Many of the operational and people challenges were very similar in these two environments. So one of the things I initiated early on to address the employee performance challenges was an annual review process that included a detailed skills and performance assessment.

The detailed skills and performance assessment was completed by each employee within the division and me separately. This enabled the individual employee (and me) to provide a written proficiency ranking on a scale of 1 to 10 for every critical performance area. During the formal review process, it also enabled us to discuss any skills or performance gaps or significant deviations in the ranking scores and then determine the appropriate actions to take.

What was interesting about this review process is in every case, marginally performing employees overestimated their performance, rarely giving themselves a score below 8 out of 10 in any area. Top performers, on the other hand, underestimated their performance and rarely gave themselves a score above 8 out of 10 in any area. Why? Top performers are always seeking ways to improve their individual performance and get better. Marginal performers have the misguided view that they are already there.

Why is competence so important?

Let's make the answer really simple. It's great to love or be passionate about what you're doing. In fact, I encourage my clients to "do what you love and love what you do." However, if you lack the knowledge, skills, abilities, or training to achieve the goal, how can you expect a successful outcome? You wouldn't attempt to parachute out of a plane without the proper training and instruction, or to fly the airplane for that matter. Right?

So let's get back to the original question. Competence is so important because without it we are nothing. I know this may sound rather harsh, but if we lack the basic knowledge, skills, abilities, etc. to achieve a certain level of competence in business or in life, what do we have to fall back on, and how can we move forward? The answer is: we can't. We're stuck in limbo until we do obtain the required abilities or someone rescues us.

So first things first, you need to get your books and acquire the appropriate knowledge, skills, and training before pressing ahead. In this fast-paced, get-it-and-go world we live in today, shrinking the learning curve on new things has become a virtual necessity and one way to stay ahead. For most areas of life, there are tangible benefits to getting better, faster and accelerating our ability to acquire new competencies and skills.

In his book, *Outliers: The Story of Success*, best-selling author Malcolm Gladwell stated that it requires ten thousand hours of practice (10,000-Hour Rule) to master a specific task. Unless you plan to become a brain surgeon or master craftsman, most of us don't have or will not devote ten thousand hours to the mastery of new things. One of the best ways to shrink the learning curve (without sacrificing quality) is to seek out a coach or mentor who has *mastered* what you're trying to accomplish to help guide you through the learning process.

> *Make the most of yourself, for that is all there is of you.*
>
> —Ralph Waldo Emerson

Although synonymous with competence, having *ability* and *knowledge* in a particular subject area does not directly translate to competence. It still requires you to *demonstrate* that ability or knowledge in meaningful ways. For example, taking the SAT exam, a test for college admission that measures intelligence, numerous times to improve your test score does not equate to competence, particularly if you still can't tie your own shoes when the exam is over. It's a rote memory exercise.

A master electrician is a good case in point of competence. To become a master electrician, you must complete five hundred to a thousand classroom hours and between eight thousand and ten thousand hours of on-the-job training (i.e., Malcom Gladwell's 10,000-Hour Rule). We show competence by *doing*. If you want to know what makes a great master electrician, athlete, teacher, or anything else, you need to go into the field and experience it firsthand.

Once we have demonstrated competence, then "How can we improve?" becomes the most fundamental and valuable question to be answered. Continuous improvement is essential to growth in all of the critical five *F* areas of life: faith, family, finances, fitness, and fun. You don't get better by staying the same. The competitive world we live in requires us to continue to advance our knowledge, skills, and abilities or risk falling behind.

Success in business and life requires a sustained commitment to growth and excellence. The desire for continuous improvement should be an integral part of what drives us to excel as individuals and as business and community leaders. If we are not focused on constantly raising the bar in terms of our expectations, our abilities, and our performances, then what is the point? And further, how do we get better?

What I always encourage is to not focus on what to do different, but rather focus on what to do better. Unfortunately, we are easily distracted by bright, shiny objects and everything that is going on around us and have a penchant for the new and improved. This can become a serious problem when we're attempting to advance our skills and build the competencies needed individually or organizationally.

As I mentioned in the beginning of this chapter, one of the keys to success at anything is being good at what you do. However, we don't get better, faster by trying to juggle too many balls at the same time or by chasing rainbows that lead us down the proverbial rabbit hole. This only results in costly mistakes and amplifies the risk of failure.

All too often, entrepreneurs fail to recognize these trappings. Rather than focusing on their core competencies and building upon them, they stretch their limited resources too thin trying to do everything. Or they overinvest in the deal of the week rather than putting more time, energy, and resources into what they do well to systematically improve the growth, profitability, and performance of their businesses.

In order to *get better*, we all have to *do better*. We will spend the next chapter discussing performance, but for now let's just say there is a direct correlation between competence and performance. In theory, the more competent we are to perform a given task, the better our performance. And the better our performance, the greater our odds of success.

Just remember, there is no secret formula for success. In all things, it takes hard work, determination, staying power, and competence to reach the pinnacle of success. Be sure you are well prepared for the opportunities and challenges ahead by taking the necessary steps to acquire the skills and competencies you'll need to be and do your best.

CHAPTER 5

Performance

Success is not *proportional to effort;* results *are.*

What do we know about performance? Well, what we should know is that performance, success, effort, and results are interrelated but not interchangeable.

Performance dictates the actions you take and how well you execute them. When we think about performance, it ultimately comes down to "how did you do?" It comes down to results.

Success is the accomplishment of an aim, goal, or purpose —the desired result.

Effort is generally thought of as a precursor to results. It's the *trying* versus the *doing*—the energy you put forth to do or attempt to do something.

Results are what you get following a series of actions. Therefore, results is the yardstick by which we *measure* our performance, our progress, and our level of success. Why do some people get confused by this?

> *Never mistake activity for achievement.*
>
> —John Wooden

A great example to illustrate this point is a golf swing. There are apparently six steps to a perfect golf swing. (I'm not a golfer.) Granted, it takes a certain amount of effort to swing a golf club. But are you going to celebrate the fact that you got all six steps in the proper order and swung the club? No. You're going to celebrate success when you hit the little white ball three hundred or more yards straight down the fairway into the hole.

Your performance is going to be measured by results not effort—not the number of steps it took you to get there or the number of calories you burned. Likewise, effort or activity will not directly translate to success. People who tend to be the most effective are able to prioritize and get the most out of their time. It's quality versus quantity or, better yet, less equals more when it comes to performance and results.

Busy being busy does not constitute an effective formula for outstanding performance and success in any field—arts, music, entertainment, sports, business, or life. (We'll address my formula for success in business later in this chapter.) This is one of the reasons I'm not a big fan of to-do lists. Why? Because they are activity-based versus results-based and contribute to busyness.

In general, what happens to most to-do lists? They are discarded or end up not being completed. Why? They include far too many items. There is no clear-cut sense of priorities. Not all of the items on the list are completed in the time frames required. And at the end of the day, the owner of the list is worn out and frustrated by the lack of progress made in reaching his or her goals.

If you feel compelled to make a list, make it a get-done-*today* list. Limit the list to the top three to five items, in priority order, for that day only. Make the completion of these items nonnegotiable. Commit to the list, stay on task, and get it done *today*.

Check out my good friend Lauren Midgley's book, *It's 6 a.m. and I'm Already Behind*, to learn more about strategies on how to get caught up in our crazy business world.

Fun fact: Your brain will perform better if you think you've slept well, even if you haven't.

When I think about *performance*, what immediately comes to mind are three things: accomplishment, execution, and results. We all want to get better, faster as I touched on in the previous chapter (and get a good night's sleep). However, many people get caught up in a firestorm of activity and equate this to accomplishment. It's not! It's the hundred pounds of poop in a fifty-pound bag phenomenon I touched on in chapter 1.

Improved performance and results can cover not only any field but also any area of life, from career, health and fitness, finances, marriage and family, our faith life, and more. So, what are some of the things to consider when seeking to improve performance and results in a specific area?

Below is my short list of things to consider when you want to improve performance and results and get better, faster in a given area.

1. Be clear on the desired performance and where you are today.
2. Have a written improvement plan with complete dates.
3. Establish realistic goals and benchmarks to monitor progress.
4. Commit to the changes that need to take place and own them.
5. Create a daily get-done-*today* list and follow it.
6. Minimize distractions and eliminate excuses.
7. Raise your level of performance to meet the expectations.
8. Solicit the support and feedback from others.
9. Celebrate your successes and keep going.

Based on your experience, feel free to add to my short list those things that will help you improve performance and results in the areas important to you.

Now what happens if I take all of the necessary steps outlined and the performance is still not where it needs to be? Then you must determine the underlying root cause(s) for the shortfall, start asking the appropriate questions, and make course corrections.

Most of the time, you will find that something was missed along the way, and you can now go back and address it. However, if there were no gaps and nothing was missed, then it's time to move to plan B; recalibrate and make adjustments to get on the right trajectory.

When we think about performance, the goal should always be to raise the bar in terms of our expectations while continuing to make steady progress. Performance improvement, therefore, is a continuum process. We don't get better by staying the same, and when we stop caring, changing and growing, we're done.

Some people want it to happen, some people wish it would happen, others make it happen.

—Michael Jordan

Want better results? Who doesn't? Every business owner is constantly seeking ways to improve performance, achieve his or her goals, and be more successful. The one common thread that connects each of us is a desire for *more*. We all desire more of something—more money, free time, sleep, etc.—which ultimately requires *more results*.

Fun fact: Lazy people accomplish more. Their laziness enables them to find the easiest and quickest ways to get things done.

There have been countless articles, books, formulas, buzz words, and antidotes devoted to the topic of "how to improve performance and get better results." From my work with hundreds of business leaders in my coaching practice and my elite mastermind program, I have found that the key to better results ultimately boils down to how well a business performs in five critical areas: people, leadership, accountability, culture, and execution.

I refer to these as the PLACE performance areas. These five areas are top of mind for most business leaders today. So, if you have struggled to get better results or make it to the next level, consider what areas to focus on to improve your PLACE performance. (Complete the following assessment to learn more.)

Check off those items (4 points each) that are currently in place from the list under each of the five PLACE performance areas. Now, add all of the checked-off items together to determine your score (0 to 20 points) in each one of the five performance categories. Finally, add the totals together from the five areas to get your total PLACE performance score (0 to 100).

PLACE Performance:

_____ People

- team members or stakeholders versus employees
- right people doing the right things
- follow the Golden Rule
- embrace diversity, openness, and change
- create opportunities for learning and growth

____ **Leadership**

- visible and engaged at all levels
- set high standards *by their example*
- empower others to succeed
- provide support where needed
- transparency in communication

____ **Accountability**

- clarity of roles and responsibilities
- ownership mentality. No monkey management
- provide 360-degree feedback
- emphasize continuous improvement and growth
- maintain a results-driven focus

____ **Culture**

- aligns with vision and core values
- create an environment of trust
- find ways to make the work fun
- high employee morale and retention
- encourage risk-taking, creativity, and innovation

____ **Execution**

- SMART goals in place
- consistently meet or exceed objectives
- deliver on promises
- customer retention is high
- learn from "perfect" failures

____ **Total PLACE performance**

So … How did you do?

Compare your total PLACE performance score with the categories in the chart provided below to determine where you are today:

100	Rock star! … What's next?
90–99	Excellent … Keep going!
80–89	Good … More work ahead.
70–79	Borderline … Pick up the pace!
< 70	Business at risk! … Take recovery action!

As mentioned earlier, improved performance and better results ultimately comes down to how well you do in these five critical areas. If you want to achieve greater success and outperform the competition, the formula is pretty straightforward:

People + Leadership + Accountability +
Culture + Execution = Results

In business and life, great results *are* the key to success. Effort, no matter how great it may be, can only take us so far. If you're serious about making success a reality, then commit the time, energy, and resources required to deliver real, tangible results and go higher.

CHAPTER 6

Authority

There will always be a Higher Power, both here and after.

When we think of a Higher Power, what are some of the things that come to mind? God, Supreme Being, Creator, boss, and wife (admit it, guys; our wives do rule the roost) are the most common things that pop up on the short list.

In terms of a High Power, God is always first on the list. Whether you are a believer or not, for purposes of this chapter, let's all agree that *we* did not get here because two rocks collided in outer space or because two apes happened to have wild monkey sex in some remote jungle. We are here due to the divine action of our Creator.

But what about authority? What is the difference between power and authority? *Power* is the ability to influence others or control their actions. *Authority* is the legal and formal right to give orders and command and enforce obedience.

While power may be express or implied, authority is direct and unequivocal.

> *If you think you have power, you have power. If you don't think you have power, you have no power.*
>
> —Michael Korda

Power affects more than individuals; it shapes larger entities such as groups, professional organizations, and governments. Similarly, a government's power is not necessarily limited to control of its own citizens. A dominant nation, for instance, will often use its power to influence or support other governments or to seize control of other territories.

Why is authority important? Because there would be anarchy and chaos without it. Authority promotes harmony and social order. Think for a moment what our lives would be like without authority and social order. It would be lawlessness and mayhem. We would be out of control, running amuck like nomads with no real sense of direction or purpose. It would be a self-destructive world much like that depicted in the movie *Mad Max*.

Growing up we're taught to respect authority—our parents and elders, the police, teachers and coaches, the military, etc. And yes, to respect our president and government officials, although this seems to have been lost in translation somewhere along the line. But today we live in a society where some people have a difficult time dealing with authority and all it represents. So what happened?

Fun fact: In America, any emails that are older than 180 days old can be read by the federal government without a warrant, although this may be changing soon under the revised privacy laws currently being addressed in Congress.

Has authority become a bad thing? Yes and no. Authority is a good thing when it promotes harmony and order and works for the common good. However, much like power, absolute authority corrupts absolutely. If the authority is dictatorial or repressive, does not work for the benefit of others, or corrupts the organization or institution it is in place to support, then it is a bad thing.

The most recent presidential campaign revealed the dark side of authority. If this is the best we can expect from our elected officials in government, then we're in big trouble. However, we are not immune from criticism either. It's time to take the high ground and distance ourselves from the political shenanigans that go on in Washington, DC, stop the preoccupation with the constantly negative news and the social media bashing that has consumed our airwaves, and take a hard look at ourselves.

> *Unthinking respect for authority is the greatest enemy of truth.*
>
> —Albert Einstein

Whether we are in a position of power and authority or not, honesty, accountability, integrity, respect, and truth should be cornerstones of our value system and what drives us to be and do better. They are also essential to a healthy respect for authority in all aspects of life. If this is still rings true, then explain to me how we have gotten so far off track as a nation and as human beings?

Our moral compass has been severely tested by the election and other recent events, and I am appalled by how poorly we have responded. As a society and individually, we have shown an unhealthy lack of regard for truth and fairness and little regard for how we treat others, particularly those in authority. This is reprehensible, and we must *all* do better.

Authority versus leadership: Without question, leadership is a hot topic in most circles today that we will cover in much more detail in chapter 14. For now, let's distinguish between authority and leadership by saying that authority is the control of others, while leadership is, or should be, about serving others. Maybe this is why some people have a problem with authority. They do not like the *control* aspect that goes with it.

In this country, there are strict laws and regulations we must adhere to, but within the framework of our society, we also enjoy a tremendous amount of freedom—freedom to choose. I do not think most people have a problem so much with authority as they do with the consequences that result from some of the bad choices they make. Our choices govern our actions, and those actions often come with negative outcomes.

If you break the law, get caught, and are punished for the crime, are the police or the court system responsible for your bad choices? No. You may not agree with all of the laws or regulations in place, but they're there for your protection. Be accountable and accept the responsibility for your actions. (This is one of the reasons I do not support the so called Platinum Rule being socialized these days.)

The Platinum Rule portends that the Golden Rule is outdated and should be replaced with do unto others as *they* would have done to them. In my opinion, this logic is flawed and violates social norms. Should we really accept someone's autonomy if they choose to do harm to others and break the law? Of course not. We don't get to pick and choose which laws or authorities we obey or disregard.

Okay, I'll get off my soapbox now. You understand the point I'm trying to make here. Let's shift gears to the positive and discuss the hierarchy of authority and why it is both necessary and valued for stability and growth. A hierarchy of authority most often exists within the government, military, and businesses, particularly larger organizations.

Fun fact: All military working dogs are ranked a level higher than their handlers to prevent the handler from mistreating the dog.

Much like a pyramid, the level of authority and responsibility increases as you rise higher within the organization. Although modern business theory promotes the flattening of the organizational model, a hierarchy of authority is designed to benefit the growth and stability of the organization and its employees.

A clearly defined hierarchy creates a path of *accountability* for every project and activity within the organization. A hierarchy of authority also helps to establish efficient communication between employees, departments, and divisions of the company. Finally, the hierarchy of authority provides a distinct career path for development, guidance, and support for each employee within the organization.

Most of us *do* develop a healthy respect for authority, and the hierarchy of authority, at an early age. I know I did. I grew up in a modest home with my parents, grandmother, and great-aunt. It was clear to me who was in charge in our household—everyone but me. It was yes, ma'am; yes, sir; mind your manners; do what you're told; or get a swat or the belt to the behind. I wasn't the brightest student, so I got my share of swats to the behind before I finally learned the lessons.

Once I learned the value of playing by the rules and the importance of respecting authority, life was pretty simple. These lessons carried over into all areas of my life from childhood through adulthood. In each of these areas, respecting authority became second nature—home, school, church, sports, career, community, etc. I didn't always agree with my marching orders; however, I fully understood the consequences if I strayed from the path or disrespected authority. These *life lessons* became particularly relevant when I assumed positions of authority as a parent, businessman, and church leader.

Are children getting these valuable life lessons today? (You be the judge here.)

Now, is it okay to question authority? The short answer is: yes. It's okay to question (not resist or defy) authority. We are human beings, and it is part of our DNA to ask questions, seek clarification, and discover the truth. Questioning leads to an open dialogue and discussion, whereby both parties can express their viewpoints. Besides, when we know the why, it becomes a teachable moment and makes it easier for us to accept the final outcome.

There will always be a Higher Power, both here and after. Accept this reality and do your part by setting the right example and respecting authority. Work within the framework of our society and play by the rules. Whether you have power, authority, or both, use it for good to make yourself and the world around you better.

Your future self and generations to come will thank you for it.

CHAPTER 7
Truthfulness

Everyone lies, just don't let tall tales become your reality.

Yes, this I know to be truth: we all lie. In fact, by the age of four, 90 percent of children have grasped the concept of lying, and it's all downhill from there. According to a study by the University of Massachusetts, 60 percent of adults can't have a ten-minute conversation without lying at least once. Most lie an average of three times during that short time span.

Fun fact: The average American lies eleven times per week. I don't lie that much, so I know some of you out there must be raising this average with all of your tall tales. (Probably a lie on my part.)

Why do we feel compelled to lie? Our environments and the people around us that we interact with daily influence us to be less than truthful. Sadly, it is a part of what makes us human and is reflected in both our business and personal lives. And the frequency with which we lie does not change much as we mature and grow older.

Okay, are there varying degrees of the truth? In classical logic, we have only two values—*true* or *false.* Therefore, when we use a system that accounts for differing degrees of truth, we refer to this as fuzzy logic. So, if we subscribe to the notion that there are differing degrees of truth, just how many are out there? The short answer is: there are an infinite number of truths.

This same logic can be applied to lies as well. How many degrees of lies are out there, and when is lying acceptable? These are two different questions. Let's start with the first one. There are numerous (probably infinite) degrees of lies from those little white ones to the big-ole whoppers that can be categorized. Some of the most common reasons we lie include:

- inflate your self-image
- fear of punishment
- cover up a mistake
- cheating on partner
- avoid conflict
- omission of facts
- protect your privacy
- gain control or influence
- hurt other people

Now to the second question: lying should never be acceptable. It is always better to tell the truth rather than risk being caught in a lie. However, there are circumstances that could arise when telling a little white lie may be viewed as okay, particularly if it enables you to avoid hurting someone's feelings or sharing inappropriate information with a child.

In fact, a study about the ethics of lying conducted several years ago by the Wharton School of the University of Pennsylvania concluded that "well-intentioned lies are considered to be moral" in today's modern society. "Individuals with altruistic intentions are perceived to be more moral, more benevolent, and more honest, *even when they lie.*"

> *O, what a tangled web we weave when first we practice to deceive.*
>
> —Walter Scott

Deception—not telling me something or hiding something on purpose—is also a form of lying. Many years ago, I wrote a poem titled "Halloween" that addressed the harmful side effects deception can cause. The poem was about a young man who was struggling to find his place in the world and discover his true identity.

One morning the young man woke up and looked in the mirror and did not recognize the image staring back at him. So he asked, "Who am I?"

> Is this the mask that I wear with family?
>
> Or the one that I wear while with friends?

Or is this the mask I wear while at work,

That captures my true feelings within?

We all wear masks. I mention this because some of our greatest lies or deceptions are often those we tell ourselves and the false personas we create based on those impressions. However, by not being our true selves consistently, regardless of the audience or context, we run the risk of someday not being able to recognize the people looking back at us in the mirror.

Fun fact: When you lie, the temperature around your nose actually rises. It's known as the Pinocchio effect.

Thomas Jefferson once wrote that, "Honesty is the first chapter in the book of wisdom." I like to keep things simple, so let's all agree that honesty is always the best policy. While the truth can be hurtful at times, it is always better to lead with it. Being recognized as a person who is honest, trustworthy, and of high moral character, rather than the opposite, is the *wise* choice.

Is there a distinction between *fact* and *truth*? Yes, absolutely. A *fact* is something that is true everywhere for everyone. It is a *reality* that cannot be logically disputed or rejected. Facts can be verified or proven using standard references or scientific experiments. For example, if I say, "Ice is cold," this can be scientifically proven by converting water to ice at 32 degrees Fahrenheit. Or you could just hold an ice cube in your hand to discover this fact firsthand.

Facts are universal and don't change according to country, culture, religion, etc. *Truth,* on the other hand, is something that is dependent upon a person's perspective and life experiences. A truth is considered by many to be broader in scope than a fact. Why? Because unlike a fact, truth takes into consideration someone's feelings or beliefs, which have no place in a fact. Truths can be subjective or changed, where facts cannot be—until proven otherwise.

> *People don't want to hear the truth because they don't want their illusions destroyed.*
>
> —Friedrich Nietzsche

Boy, oh boy, does this quote perfectly reflect a day in the life of what we read and hear happening within the confines of the divisive political framework currently residing in Washington, DC, and the constantly negative daily news reports from the main stream media. It's mind-boggling.

In the movie *Shooter,* Ned Beatty plays a corrupt senator. In a clandestine meeting with a mercenary colonel, played by Danny Glover, Beatty says to him, "The truth is what I say it is." This pretty much sums up the philosophy that far too many people have adopted. We each see the world through a different lens based on our experiences.

Most of us filter what we hear, see, and read from our life experiences, personal biases, or frame of reference at any given point in time. Unfortunately, this is where fuzzy logic and fake news have taken root and begun to chip away at honesty, integrity, and trust.

> *People seldom improve when they have no other model but themselves to copy.*
>
> —Oliver Goldsmith

My favorite habit from Stephen Covey's great book, *The 7 Habits of Highly Effective People,* is habit five: "Seek first to understand, then to be understood." This could very well be an anthem for today's world. Communication is the most important skill we learn in life, and we spend years learning to read, write, and speak. But what about listening and caring about the feelings of others?

How do we avoid the temptation to spread lies, rumors, and misinformation as a result of our personal biases, perceptions, and attitudes? Adopt these basic guiding principles in your fair treatment and regard for others. In the immortal words of Marcus Aurelius, sixteenth emperor of the Roman Empire, "If it's not true, don't say it. If it's not right, don't do it."

We are all reasonably intelligent people, so seek understanding first. I am not saying you should fact check everything via Snopes.com before sharing, but do stay informed. If it sounds like a lie, half-truth, or just plain bullshit, don't put it in your mouth. And the next time something is shared with you that doesn't pass the sniff test, don't infect others by sharing it. Discard it.

The best thing about telling the truth is that you don't have to remember what you said.

—Mark Twain

What are the basic tenets for a happy, fulfilling, and productive life? I touched on them a littler earlier. Honesty, integrity, and truthfulness should be at the top of the list.

The truth comes naturally, but lying takes effort. I don't know about you, but I try to keep my tall tales to a minimum because I don't have a great memory, although my adult children would probably disagree with me on this point. Not telling the truth does have a cumulative effect and adds stress to our already stressful lives. It also moves us further away from the people we were meant to be.

Think of it this way. God made each of us to be an original, not a copy. Every time we tell a lie or misrepresent the truth, we are sacrificing a part of us—a part that makes us different and unique from each other. If you habitually lie, then eventually all of what makes you special will be gone and replaced by a lesser copy.

Never allow tall tales to become your reality. Stay true to yourself. When you have the choice between the truth and a lie, choose *wisely*. Don't become a cheap imitation of the original. Be the *best you* instead.

CHAPTER 8

Indecision

Stay on the fence long enough, and success will pass you by.

Decision-making is the process of identifying and choosing alternatives based on the values, preferences, and beliefs of the decision maker. It is the process of choosing the best among the different alternatives. In psychology, *decision-making* is regarded as the cognitive process resulting in the selection of a belief or a course of action among several alternative possibilities.

Everything in life comes down to the choices we make. What people often tend to forget is that *indecision* is also a decision—a decision that produces no action or a negative result.

What? I know this can be confusing. Here's an example: if you stand on the railroad tracks with a train approaching, indecision might cause you to not take action in order to avoid being struck, thus producing a negative result.

Aren't procrastination and indecision the same thing?

Not exactly. *Procrastination* is the *intentional* act of delaying or postponing something. It is the avoidance of a task that needs to be accomplished, and (be honest) the majority of us have become experts in the fine art of procrastination or creative avoidance. This is particularly true when it comes to putting off things we don't enjoying doing, such as laundry, housecleaning, yard work, studying, etc.

Indecision, although akin to procrastination, is an inability to make a decision in a timely manner. Most often, indecision is a psychological impairment born out of fear or a need for certainty, rather than being an intentional action. Pathological indecisiveness, or aboulomania, can severely impact decision-making and adversely affect many areas of a person's life.

Fun fact: Your brain requires glucose in order to make good decisions.

Why is decision-making so important? I know what you're probably thinking. Is this a real question? Making decisions is vitally important because we make literally thousands of them daily, both good and bad ones. According to various sources on the internet, an adult makes thirty-five thousand conscious decisions a day. This may sound like a crazy number, but according to Cornell University researchers, we make 226.7 decisions a day about food alone.

Decision-making is an integral part of life, learning, and the maturation process as a whole, beginning in early childhood. (The average child makes roughly three thousand decisions each day.) It is an art that is learned based on our life experiences and further developed and refined throughout our lifetimes. Effective decision-making is also a vital part of any business and a key function of its success.

When you come to a fork in the road, take it.

—Yogi Berra

This is one of my all-time favorite quotes and so appropriate for a discussion about indecision. During my professional career, I have been blessed to work with hundreds of business leaders, both locally and globally. One of the things that has always confounded me is decision-making reluctance. Sure, I understand risk tolerance. However, even when presented with the supporting data, many business leaders fail to take action on major initiatives that would ensure the longer-term viability and success of their businesses.

Why is making decisions so hard if we make literally thousands of them on a daily basis? There are a variety of reasons for why making decisions can be difficult. Here are some of the more common reasons for indecision I have encountered:

- fear of failure or success
- self-limiting beliefs
- too many options
- lack of motivation or direction

- desire for perfection
- stress and anxiety
- overthinking

Unfortunately, nothing changes until we are willing to take some form of action and put forth the effort required to get off the fence and affect a change. Without action, success cannot be achieved, and in many instances, failure is the end result.

Fun fact: Shy people tend to avoid taking risks, which also makes them better at making crucial, life-altering decisions.

From my perspective, the biggest hurdles to overcome when we think about the things that most often hold us back are the fear of failure or success and overthinking. So let's address each of them in a little more detail.

First, the fear of failure or success: Fear of failure (*atychiphobia*) is essentially a fear of shame. We conjure up all of these terrible things that can happen if we make the wrong decision. Consequently, we sabotage ourselves by indecision to avoid them.

The best way to overcome the fear of failure is to accept the reality that we all fail and treat it as a learning experience and not a disaster of epic proportions. Two things I stress with clients to help them overcome this issue is to first apply the 10 Percent Rule to everything. Don't focus on the 10 percent that doesn't go exactly as planned; instead, focus your energy and resources on the 90 percent that does in order to achieve an even better outcome. Second, have a plan

B just in case your plan A is derailed. These are simple but effective solutions.

> *The road of life is paved with flat squirrels who couldn't make a decision.*
>
> —Unknown

A fear of success is a little different animal and harder to overcome than a fear of failure. Why? Because we often undermine our efforts without knowing it. Unlike failure, success has the potential to have a much larger impact on our lives and the lives of the people around us. Equally important, success denotes change, and we all know how we feel about change, right? Success also forces us to move out of our comfort zones, and we don't like to be uncomfortable. Ugh!

Many of us are afraid of success. To overcome this fear, we must first recognize that it exists. Next, to get comfortable with the idea of success, visualize what it looks like. What's different? How am I different? What will I have to change to achieve success? How will success impact others—family, friends, coworkers, etc.? Keep in mind as you work through this mental exercise that no risk means no reward. Finally, am I willing to make the commitment to overcome my fear of success and actually pursue it?

Second, overthinking: Also called paralysis by analysis, this is exactly what it means—thinking too much. This is particularly true in the business world where many businesses have gone under because they overanalyzed their circumstances rather than pulling the trigger and taking action when and where needed. In Malcolm Gladwell's recent book *Blink*, he makes an argument that our split-second decision-making capabilities are far more accurate and fined-tuned than using a more drawn-out, analytical process.

How do we stop overthinking?

Overthinking can be debilitating and stressful. Beyond recognition, an important step to overcome overthinking it is to acknowledge that none of us can predict the future. So, playing out all of the possible scenarios in our heads of what could happen is a waste of time. Stop it! Next, set boundaries and time limits on making important decisions, so you don't get bogged down. Finally, quit waiting for the perfect answer. Just do your best with the information available to you and be grateful for whatever comes as a result.

How can we get better at making decisions and avoid indecision creeping in?

If you're stuck at this point in your life, there is an abundance of recommended antidotes out there to overcome obstacles in this area. When I did further research on the topic of indecision, a number of things came to light, beyond what I shared previously. You can boil all of these down to a few common themes:

1. Spend more time in the present moment.
2. Realize you cannot control everything.

3. Be patient. (This is a tough one for me.)
4. Listen to your inner voice.
5. Trust your instincts.
6. Don't be afraid to make mistakes.
7. Solicit advice from others.

I believe true progress is possible when we're able to accept our circumstances, both good and bad, for what they are—a part of life's journey. Conversely, we become our own worst enemies when we fail to recognize that our lack of action can have harmful consequences and move us further away from success.

> *Time is the coin of your life, and only you can determine how it will be spent.*
>
> —Carl Sandburg

As I touched on at the beginning of the chapter, every decision-making process produces a final choice, which may or may not prompt action. There are three simple rules to keep in mind the next time you are stuck or struggling to make an important decision and take action:

1. If you do not go after what you want, you'll never have it.
2. If you do not ask, the answer will always be no.
3. If you do not step forward, you'll always be in the same place.

Making decisions doesn't have to be a mind-numbing process. It really boils down to two things: commitment and taking action. You can never succeed unless you take action. What you will discover by taking action is that success has always been there. You just didn't recognize it before.

At the end of the day, the only bad decision is indecision. You clearly don't want to end up being a flat squirrel on the road of life. So get off the fence and get in the game. Because success is never an accident. It's always a choice, and failure is *not* an option!

CHAPTER 9

Motivation

Hugs and kudos are great, but a kick in the pants works too!

Does the quote above still apply in these modern times? Not so much.

This is one of those topics that I could go on about for days. Fortunately for my readers, I made a conscious decision to keep each chapter of the book to around 1,500 words, so you won't fall asleep on me.

Motivation is one of the most talked about and written about subjects on the planet. It is a huge topic in the business world and personal development arena. Today there are a litany of books, self-help programs, seminars, speeches, antidotes, quotes, and hyperboles devoted to motivation. However, talking about it and writing about it do little to move the needle and get us going.

The fact that you're not where you want to be should be motivation enough, right? In most cases, unfortunately, it's not. Motivation comes from within and is derived from one of two things: seeking pleasure or pain avoidance. In fact, all decisions we humans make are to avoid pain or to seek pleasure. Oddly enough, we will do much more to avoid pain (ergo, a kick in the pants) than to gain pleasure.

> *We are what we repeatedly do. Excellence, therefore, is not an act but a habit.*
>
> —Aristotle

On average, it takes roughly sixty-six days to form a new habit. However, most people in the fast-paced global society we are part of today have the attention span of a three-year-old. So, it is very difficult to move from start to finish on anything that requires a substantial time commitment to achieve excellence or mastery and become habit-forming.

Holding our attention for sixty-six days is really, really hard unless … What? Unless it is important enough to us that we're willing to make the level of commitment required to see it through and effect a *change*. Even when we know how important making the change could be to our future health and well-being, it's difficult to take that first step. Just ask anyone struggling with an addiction.

The hardest part of accomplishing anything is starting. Think about it. It's true for even a simple task like mowing the grass. We will find ways to creatively avoid starting the lawn mower until the grass is overgrown. The task of mowing the lawn in and of itself is not all that difficult once we get going. In fact, taking the time out to enjoy the fresh air, sunshine, and a little exercise is good for us.

Starting will always be difficult, as mentioned earlier, unless it's important enough to us that we will not only start but complete the task. Mowing grass is just not a *priority* for most of us, so we procrastinate and find other things to occupy our time. So, what is the priority?

What is your Wild Rabbit?

In your drive to accomplish your goals and achieve success, stop and ask yourself: what is it that I'm reaching for? Each of us has that one *big thing* we are chasing—for example, weight loss and better health, the elusive soul mate, a bigger home, that next promotion, hair restoration (oh, that's mine), etc. What is yours? More importantly, what's your motivation for reaching it?

The wild rabbit is a metaphor for one's inner drive to succeed. It is a universal symbol for the relentless pursuit of achievement for every individual. It's about mastery and going beyond in setting the standards for excellence, reaching for something bigger in your life, and not settling for the status quo. If you have read some of my blog articles on the topic of goal setting, you know I have a strong bias toward action and results. Goal setting is a total waste of time unless you're committed to taking action and making the changes necessary to achieve results.

Also, it's important to note that pursuing your one big thing (wild rabbit) and chasing rabbits are two very different things. In my coaching practice, I have encountered a lot of busy professionals who have spent an inordinate amount of time, energy, and resources chasing rabbits with little to show for their efforts.

Fun fact: Telling yourself "I can do better" is actually one of the best ways to make yourself do better at a given task.

We can *all* do better. That is why true progress and growth is a continuum process, much like motivation. So, how do we stay motivated and avoid chasing rabbits and those bright, shiny objects that can impede our progress and negatively impact motivation?

The following are what I believe to be the seven keys to getting motivated and staying there.

1. Know your why. What is your motivation? Have a clear understanding of your goals, and what needs to change to reach them, before you launch.
2. Get started now. It's impossible to reach that pinnacle of success unless you take the first step. Make it a *priority* and get going!
3. *Live* your plan. Don't just develop it. Make it a part of your daily routine. Visualize the finish line and see yourself enjoying the fruits of all your hard work.
4. Positive self-talk. Stop being your own worst critic. Delete the negative thoughts once and for all. Start being your greatest fan.

5. Set high standards. Aim high but establish goals that are realistic, specific, and measurable. You'll be amazed at what can be accomplished.
6. Monitor your progress. Be sure to routinely check in to see how you're doing and to make course corrections where needed.
7. Keep it going! To achieve excellence at anything, you need to keep moving forward and find ways to get better every day.

According to Dr. Anders Ericsson, motivation is the most significant predictor of success. "High motivation will ensure total preparation which will, in turn, ensure maximum performance and results."

Fun fact: Exercising regularly can help you to become more creative and smarter. Who knew all those hard bodies at the gym were actually raising their IQs every time they worked out. Now I know why I always feel smarter after a trip to the fitness center. Here I thought it was just the endorphins kicking in.

What are the most effective motivators in our modern world?

Whether it's developing high-performing teams in business, high-achieving children in our personal lives, or working on ourselves, the carrot works better than the stick. The days of fear and intimidation as a motivator, as depicted in the movie *Death of a Salesman*, are over. People will either tune you out and shut down or tell you to go to hell and leave.

Telling someone he or she is lazy and will never amount to anything is not the best approach either.

In the modern world, there is no one-size-fits-all solution when it comes to motivation. Every person is different in this respect. In his best-selling book *Drive*, Daniel Pink states that "people perform best when given autonomy, opportunity for mastery, and the belief their task is meaningful."

While I certainly concur with Pink's assessment, I would broaden these findings somewhat to also include the following:

1. Find out what motivates them as individuals.
2. Treat them as valued members of the team.
3. Make sure they fully understand the *why*.
4. Clarify roles, responsibilities, and expectations upfront.
5. Encourage open communication and feedback.
6. Follow up on tasks and provide support where needed.
7. Provide the appropriate recognition and rewards.

Remember … whether it's motivating your child to clean his or her room or an employee to complete an assigned project, it has to be important to that person. Otherwise, it won't get done, be done on time, or be completed in a quality manner. Something will always be missed if it's not important to me and my contributions are not valued.

Make the most of yourself, for that is all there is of you.

—Ralph Waldo Emerson

Each of us has the capacity to change, to grow, and to accomplish great things within our lifetimes. However, we cannot get better if we stay the same. We must continue to move the needle in order to get there. This is why highly motivated people tend to be more successful. They recognize that motivation and change are an integral part of growth, and they move the needle.

What motivates and inspires you to be and do your best?

Joe Namath, nicknamed Broadway Joe, was an outstanding (and colorful) NFL quarterback who led the New York Jets to the Super Bowl championship in 1969. His favorite saying at the time was, "I can't wait until tomorrow 'cause I get better looking every day!" Whatever is needed to create this kind of energy and enthusiasm is what you should capitalize on to propel you forward.

To avoid a kick in the pants, be like Joe Namath: get excited about your future and the opportunities and challenges that are ahead for you. If you want a better body, bigger house, better life, etc., you know what you need to do. Go for it!

Stay focused and surround yourself with like-minded people with similar goals who will help keep you motivated and inspire you to make your life greater than the sum of its parts.

CHAPTER 10

Purpose

A train can't move in two directions at the same time, neither can you.

Pick one!

Who am I? Why am I here? What's my motivation? What is my *why*? These are purpose-related questions most of us will struggle with at various stages throughout our lives

What is purpose, and why is it important?

Purpose is the reason anything is done, created, or exists. Everyone has or needs a purpose; otherwise, we are just flopping around with no true sense of direction or meaning to our lives. However, defining our purpose in meaningful terms can be a major challenge. This is a partial explanation for why I struggled mightily with the development of this chapter. Ironic, huh?

We quite often hear the phase "find your purpose." Every time I hear this I want to respond, "I didn't know it was lost." But in reality, it wasn't lost because in order to be found it had to exist. Therein lies the difficulty for many people.

> *If you don't know where you are going, any road will take you there.*
>
> —Lewis Carroll

Why having a purpose is important:

- focus
- clarity
- meaning
- drive and passion
- achieve success

These are just a few of the things that come to mind when we consider why having a strong sense of purpose is so important. But what else should we consider? Well for starters ...

Are motivation and purpose the same thing?

No. However, motivation and purpose are intertwined, which is why I devoted a separate chapter to each. Motivation is situational. It is what drives us toward a specific goal. To distinguish the two, purpose is universal; it is our reason for being. Without a clear sense of purpose, what is my motivation? A sense of purpose is the *fuel* that drives motivation.

In the business world, we need to similarly differentiate purpose from *vision* and *mission*. Much the same as with goals and plans, we often use these three terms interchangeably to convey the same thing. They are not.

Vision is the most powerful motivator in an organization. A vision statement describes the company's ideal future. It answers the question, "What impact do we want to have on society?" The vision is how you look after you have achieved your mission.

Mission is what you want to achieve today and in the future. The mission statement describes the overall framework of the company: *what* you do, *who* you do it for, and *how* you do it. It also establishes the boundaries for the organization's current activities.

Here are the vision and mission statements from my business, Tres Coaching Services™, to provide you with some examples:

Vision Statement:

We help clients achieve the results to move beyond their vision.

Mission Statement:

Become trusted business advisors by helping clients dramatically improve the growth, profitability, and performance of their businesses. Deliver professional coaching, education, and speaking services that consistently exceed the client's expectations.

Purpose is *why* you do what you do. Much like vision, purpose connects the head with the heart. What I mean by this is that purpose works best when it reflects your *why* as an organization. Purpose also keeps you focused on why you exist.

While most companies have developed vision and mission statements for their organizations, few have gone beyond this to look at a purpose statement even though having a strong sense of purpose tends to resonate well with customers. Regardless, having purpose and meaning are critical for any business to succeed.

> *The two most important days in your life are the day you are born and the day you find out why.*
>
> —Mark Twain

Now let's get back to purpose and you. I love this quote by Mark Twain because it really speaks to purpose. From the time of our birth until the end, everything in between is where life happens, as I mentioned in chapter 1. It reflects those collective life experiences that help us define not only who we are but what drives us.

From my perspective, purpose encapsulates not only who and what we are all about but, more importantly, what we are called to do. Living with a sense of purpose means living life to the fullest and becoming all we are meant to be in the process. When your life is driven by a clear sense of purpose, it takes on a different meaning.

Ways to live a purpose-driven life:

1. Discover your passions.
2. Live in the moment.
3. Enjoy the little things.
4. Always be kind.
5. Experience the world.
6. Help someone in need.
7. Make a difference.

Many of the above may seem to be altruistic for a reason. Living a purpose-driven life is really about a higher calling, rather than just putting in our time here on planet earth and existing day to day.

We all want to believe that our lives have purpose and what we do is recognized and valued. It's only when we stop trying and stop moving forward in our quest to attain success and personal fulfillment that we fail. As Richard St. John reminded us in his 2009 TED Talk, "Success is a continuous journey, a journey that begins with our first step."

Fun fact: Studies have shown that when people are contributing to a higher purpose, they are likely to have a healthier outlook on life and be more resilient to stress.

Now we are getting to the true essence of purpose. What is important to us in our twenties and thirties is different than what's important in our fifties and beyond. Although our goals, core values, and beliefs tend to shift over time with more life experiences, they should always be aligned with our purpose. Otherwise, we can easily become discouraged, frustrated, and lost.

Maslow's hierarchy of needs is a good example for how our priorities shift during various stages of our lives. Maslow's hierarchy of needs is a theory of motivation developed by Abraham Maslow. Maslow believed people move through different stages of five needs that motivate our behavior:

1. Physiological: food, shelter, clothing
2. Safety: financial security, health, wellness
3. Social: love, family, friendship, community
4. Esteem: accomplishment, respect, personal worth
5. Self-actualization: self-awareness, personal growth, fulfillment

Normally, the hierarchy of needs is displayed as a pyramid in ascending order. Numbers 1 and 2 on the bottom levels of the pyramid are commonly referred to as the basic needs. As we move up the pyramid, our sense of purpose comes into play, particularly in numbers 4 and 5. This is also where we begin to focus more on those higher level goals, such as serving others, making a difference, and leaving a legacy.

When we are connected to something greater than ourselves, we tend to have a greater sense of purpose in our lives, and our core values and beliefs will reflect this change. Bob Buford addresses this time of transition as a growing awareness in midlife "moving from success to significance" in his book *Halftime: Moving from Success to Significance.*

> *Unless you assume a God, the question of life's purpose is meaningless.*
>
> —Bertrand Russell, Atheist

Speaking of connecting to something greater than ourselves, I'll close out this chapter by letting you in on a little secret. The reason we so often struggle with purpose is this: It's not about us. Focusing on ourselves will never reveal the true purpose of our lives.

Christian author Rick Warren wrote the book titled *The Purpose Driven Life* in 2002. In the most recent special edition of his book, Warren points out that, "The purpose of life has puzzled people for thousands of years. That's because we typically begin at the wrong starting point—ourselves."

As Warren writes, "The purpose of your life is far greater than your own personal fulfillment, your peace of mind, and even your happiness. It's far greater than your family, your career, and even your wildest dreams and ambitions. If you want to know why you were placed on this planet, you must begin with God. You were born *by* his purpose and *for* his purpose."

Routinely, I take what I refer to as 5k faith walks when I'm struggling with a problem and seeking divine guidance and direction. Now, if you want to learn more about my purpose, my *why*, you can find it on my blog site in an article titled, "John's Story." I share this as a side note because one of the great ways to help discover your purpose is by writing your story.

Trying to discover your life's purpose can be confusing, frustrating, and overwhelming at times, particularly when the answers are not forthcoming. If you are having difficulty in this area, it may be helpful to spend some time away from the daily rat race and do some soul-searching, journaling, or praying.

You may never get the answers you seek to all of those burning questions. However, developing a closer relationship with our Lord and Savior and serving others, whether you are ten or one hundred years old, should be a priority if you want to live a purpose-driven life.

CHAPTER 11
Self-Doubt

You can't see the light at the end of the tunnel with the covers pulled over your head.

Self-doubt and self-limiting beliefs are major stumbling blocks and buzzkills for many of us. So, where shall we begin? I guess as good a place as any is to acknowledge that we are all victims of self-doubt and have self-limiting beliefs. In fact, self-doubt and self-limiting beliefs are ingrained in each of us from early childhood.

What is the difference between self-limiting beliefs and self-doubt?

Self-limiting beliefs are beliefs that constrain us in some way. These beliefs are about ourselves and our own identities, as opposed to other people and the world around us. Self-limiting beliefs are what prevent us from living our best lives and lead to self-doubt. *Self-doubt*, on the other hand, is a lack of confidence in yourself and your abilities. Self-doubt robs us of our joy and stifles our creativity, growth, and development.

Fun fact: It's been said that most infants function at a genius level until age one.

From early childhood on, our ability to process and absorb the vast amount of information and knowledge we are bombarded with begins to slow significantly. By adulthood, there are few of us who can truly be called geniuses (present company included). If there is any truth to this decline in cognitive function or mental acuity—i.e., reasoning, memory, attention, and language—then what is the cause?

Our well-meaning parents are one of the major contributors. It's true! According to Dr. Cynthia Thaik, "The steady and rapid decline in this high-level cognitive function is the learned behavior of self-doubt and self-judgement, often imposed on us by meaningful parents." Just think back for a moment to those times growing up when you were told you couldn't do something because you were too short, not smart enough, or not pretty enough or because it was too expensive or too dangerous and so forth.

While many of those well-meaning comments sheltered us from harm, they also created boundaries that held us back from experiencing life on our terms. My father's hurtful words to me from my early childhood—"You're lazy and will never amount to anything"—still ring in my ears today in weaker moments. During my youth, I bought into them and was a classic underachiever.

However, these *self-imposed* limitations did not deter me from pursuing my hopes and dreams for a better life. As I grew older and more experienced, I turned those negative words into a positive and used them as fuel to help inspire me to accomplish more than I ever dreamed possible.

> *When you change the way you look at things, the things you look at change.*
>
> —Dr. Wayne W. Dyer

If you are unhappy with your life's direction and have grown tired of beating yourself up or are continually questioning your motives and actions, then it's time to change things up. Beyond the obvious of eliminating negative self-talk, here are a few of my thoughts on how to change the way you look at things and break the cycle of self-doubt.

Top Five *Don't* List:

1. Sell yourself short anymore. Replace "I can't" with "I can" and put your energy and time into the things you are truly passionate about. Each morning before you get out of bed, finish this phrase: "I'm the very best at …"
2. Beat yourself up over past mistakes or disappointments. It's hard to move forward if you're still holding on to the baggage from the past. Life is too short; it's time to turn the page and move on to the brighter future ahead for you.
3. Wait until tomorrow to catch lightning in a bottle. Make *now* your favorite word. Do the little things

that must be done every day to move forward, reach your goals, and achieve success.

4. Miss a single opportunity to say the words "I love you" and "thank you" to all of the special people in your life. Love and gratitude can and will go a long way to cure an ailing heart, mind, or spirit.
5. Sweat the small stuff. In the grand scheme of things, it really is *all* small stuff. So, just enjoy the ride!

Top Five *Do* List:

1. Devote more time to the five *F*'s: faith, family, finances, fitness, and fun. Enjoy the blessings and embrace the challenges each new day brings in these most important areas of your life.
2. Get out of your way. Really start to enjoy *your life*. Be passionate about where you are right now and celebrate your daily accomplishments, both large and small.
3. Make a difference. Put your time, talents, and resources to work to improve yourself and the world around you. Pursue new projects, opportunities, and challenges with enthusiasm.
4. Be a better spouse, parent, colleague, neighbor, and friend. Broaden your horizons and meet new people, build new relationships and partnerships, and lend a helping hand to others in need of your expertise, guidance, or support.
5. Learn to live with the *real* you. But don't just live. Truly enjoy being you. Embrace your flaws and

learn to laugh at yourself. Life's not perfect and neither are you, so get on with it!

Fun fact: Talking to yourself actually makes you smarter.

Before we move on, let's spend a little more time on negative self-talk because it's a major impediment to our growth and development. We have all heard and listened to the I'm-not-worthy voice in our heads from time to time. When you hear that negative voice start to grow louder, do what I do. *Change the channel.* Just say, "Stop it!" and then turn it to the positive. For example, if your inner voice is telling you that you're not qualified for the next big job you applied for, say, "Stop it!"

Now, reframe the conversation by saying, "I'm grateful for the opportunity to compete for this new position. Given my background and experience, I know I can be a great asset to the organization in this or other positions I may be considered for in the future." Changing the tenor of the inner conversation will not assure you of getting that next big job you are seeking; however, feeling good about yourself and having a positive outlook can't hurt.

> *You don't drown by falling in water. You drown by staying there.*
>
> —Edwin Louis Cole

Self-doubt breeds procrastination, and it can have a paralyzing effect on the mind that results in the covers-over-the-head syndrome. Left unchecked, self-doubt can lead us to question our self-worth or become stuck and unable to move forward. If this happens to you, here are six things you can do to help get unstuck and moving forward again:

1. Change your routine. Start with the little things—for example, take a different route to the office or check email later in the day rather than the first thing in the morning. Then build from there to find creative and expansive ways to get outside your comfort zone and develop solutions to overcome the challenges that have been holding you back.
2. Adjust your vision. The I-can't-see-the-light-at-the-end-of-the-tunnel mentality can be overcome by simply adjusting your vision. When you're stuck, you have a tendency to look at your shoe tops rather than what is ahead of you. Stay focused on the bigger picture and don't allow yourself to get distracted by the events of the day or minor setbacks.
3. Move away from the problem. I refer to this as the out-of-body approach. When clients hit the wall, I encourage them to examine their *reactions* to determine what changes they need to make to get back on the right track. Remember: life is 10 percent what happens to us and 90 percent how we react to it.
4. Take a day off to decompress. Similar to number 1, sometimes all it takes is a day away from the normal routine to get your motor running and the creative juices flowing again. Grab some of your buddies for a round of golf or your gal pals for a day of retail

therapy. You will be amazed at the difference it will make in your mental outlook.

5. Go visit your best customers or friends. There is nothing more invigorating than spending time with your best peeps when you need an energy boost. They are a great source of positivity, as well as a great resource for new ideas and approaches to help you stay grounded. Take them to lunch and enjoy the time together.
6. Seek expert advice. Sometimes getting unstuck requires professional support from someone (a coach, mentor, trusted advisor, or pastor) who has the desired expertise in a specific area and who can bring a fresh perspective to help you to identify and overcome the source of the problem.

Self-doubt is one of the major obstacles to living the life you so richly deserve. Many of you have sold yourself short in the past because of negative life experiences similar to mine. Don't let them define you.

Above all, don't let the opinions and comments of others, even well-meaning parents, hold you back. Find a way to rise above them, so you can start living your best life right now and become the person you were meant to be.

CHAPTER 12
Reality

There are no *guarantees, only opportunities.*

Would you like to start over?

Wow ... What a loaded question, huh? Let's be totally honest. We have all had days, weeks, months, and perhaps even years that we wish we could do over. It's human nature for us to want to go back and change things that didn't go well or take back things we said, did, or didn't do we later regretted—like missed opportunities.

Quite frankly, I think it is one of the reasons we humans are so enamored with the idea of time travel. The opportunity to go back in time and right the wrongs done to us, erase those bad occurrences, or redo the swings and misses that left a stain upon our otherwise perfect lives. Just hit the reset button and start over.

And why not? Computers have reset buttons, so do most smart devices today. Heck, in the game of golf, there are a number of opportunities to make up for bad or missed shots. Let's see, there are gimmes, mulligans, ball drops, etc. So, why not we humans?

Where's our reset button?

Unfortunately, there are no do-overs in real life. No time travel, no gimmes, mulligans, etc. that would allow us to autocorrect or avoid life's imperfections altogether. There is only living each day we have been given to the fullest, regardless of the outcome. No guarantees, only opportunities.

Besides, what we have learned about time travel from sci-fi movies tells us that going back in time and altering the past would cause a ripple effect and do more harm than good.

> *If you're looking for that one person who can change your life, take a look in the mirror.*
>
> —Marilyn Monroe

Let's talk for a moment about the *big lie*. The big lie is what we tell ourselves when we've had a bad day or when things aren't going the way we had hoped: "Things are going to get better." They're not. Things are not going to get better until what? Until you do. It's the simple truth.

The only thing we are given is an *opportunity* for a better life. After that, there are no guarantees. You're not guaranteed a great family, education, career, home, health care, or anything else. If you want those things, you need to *earn* them through dedication and hard work. Being born into the right family can help too.

However, there is a certain segment of the population that has the misguided belief you can just show up and be given all of these things. It's your right as a human being. Wrong!

The reality is it's not a level playing field, and in the end, someone always has to write the check and pay for it. You can absolutely have the great life you have always dreamed about … if you're willing to make the *commitment* and *sacrifices* necessary to achieve it.

> *Nobody can go back and start a new beginning, but anyone can start today and make a new ending.*
>
> —Maria Robinson

Rather than feeling compelled to search for the reset button or expecting someone to just *gift* us something, what should we do instead to get back on the right track when things are not working out as planned?

Here are five thoughts to consider:

1. This is not the end. What is happening to you right now, good or bad, is temporary, not an end-of-days event. Don't allow it to consume your life.

2. No one is immune. We will all face disappointments and adversity on some level in our lifetimes. Don't shrink from it when it strikes. Take corrective action and find strength by working through it.
3. Eliminate negative self-talk (chapter 11). No matter how difficult the journey might seem, there are millions of people around the world who would trade places with you in a heartbeat.
4. No pity parties or blame games. Avoid the common tendency to feel sorry for yourself when things don't go your way or to point fingers at others. Keep in mind that we are 100 percent responsible for our own happiness, no one else.
5. Focus on the *now*. Don't allow those bad things that have affected you in the past to become a part of your future reality. Leave the past where it belongs.

Fun fact: Excuses will always be there for you. Opportunity won't.

Are your expectations aligned with reality?

None of us grew up with the notion of being average, just being good enough. Whether in sports, music, grades, or business, we have all been ingrained with the idea of being the best in our chosen pursuits. Does this seem realistic? There is nothing wrong with the quest for excellence. However, not everyone can be a top performer. Real life just doesn't work that way.

Statistically, the majority of us, roughly 60 percent, fall into the normal or average range, whether we accept this as our lot in life or not. So, average really isn't a bad thing. And it certainly does not imply that if you are average, you should stop trying to improve. It's simply an indicator of how you stack up when compared with your peer group at any given point in time, which can change.

Now, what if adversity or bad things that happened to us are not what we want to autocorrect and do over? What if it is missed opportunities instead? We have all played the what-if game, right? What a terrible waste of our most precious resource—time. Playing the what-if game only moves us further away from the opportunities that are right in front of us today.

In the business world, we assess risk and opportunity cost frequently in determining the business direction and investment decisions. Many of these trade-offs result in missed opportunities. Directly or indirectly, we do the same thing with those thirty-five thousand decisions we make each day, evaluating one course of action versus another.

In doing so, we create our own reality and happiness. To that point, I believe opportunities begin to appear when we accept our circumstances, both good and bad, for what they are—a part of life's journey. Ask yourself this: "Is today the day?" The day you take the first step toward making the life changes required to enable your goals and dreams to become a reality?

Is this day one or just another day? The choice is yours and yours alone. Will this be a day of celebration or another day to rush through to the finish line? Better still, is this *the day* you decide to make something extraordinary happen and …

1. Let go of the past hurt and start to heal?
2. Tell someone you care about how much you love them?
3. Start the new business you've always wanted?
4. Make an offer on your future home?
5. Begin planning for a new addition to the family?
6. Renew wedding vows with the love of your life?
7. Join a church and affirm your faith?
8. Purchase tickets for that dream vacation?
9. Start a diet and exercise program—and stick with it?
10. Trade in your old car for a new one?
11. Extend the hand of friendship to someone in need?
12. Become the best version of you?

Don't allow yourself to get too comfortable with the status quo and let the life-changing opportunities that are in front of you slip away. Start to work on those bucket list items—today. Don't put them off! Because life changes with each step we take.

Fun fact: Friday increases the happiness all around the world by 11 percent.

While you're working on those new opportunities and bucket-list items, be sure to also make time to identify what you are grateful for and declare it.

Even in the darkest times, we can find a way through them by expressing gratitude for the good things in our lives rather than dwelling on the negatives. Life is not always fair. However, as Joel Osteen so aptly points out, "When we dwell on painful experiences in our past, our emotions go right back there with us."

We can choose to be *bitter* when things don't go our way, or we can get *better* by recognizing there is always a reason to be grateful. It is our choice to make.

Start each day by saying aloud what you are grateful for and then show it through your attitude and by caring for others. *Pay it forward.* The next time you're not feeling that attitude of gratitude for all your blessings, consider this: 71 percent of the world's population lives on less than ten dollars a day. Your life could be much worse, and these statistics help to put things into perspective.

A part of living a meaningful life is accepting the fact that meaningful does not mean *perfect.* However, despite our circumstances, we all have the capacity to change, to grow, and to accomplish great things.

By moving beyond adversity, disappointments, and regret, we will be in a much better position to capitalize on the opportunities that do come our way and get the most out of our lives.

CHAPTER 13

Forgiveness

Whoever said, "love means never having to say you're sorry," was from a galaxy far, far away!

Boy this is a tough one for many of us, isn't it?

Letting go of hurt, anger, and/or the feeling of betrayal can be difficult. Rather than forgiveness, our initial *reaction* is to lash out in anger or to seek revenge in order to right the wrong done to us. The Bible tells us we should turn the other cheek, but more often than not, we want to roll up our fist and punch the evil wrongdoer.

Why is it so easy to hold a grudge?

Human behavior being what it is suggests that we are hardwired to retaliate when we have been hurt by another person. What we fail to recognize is the person we are really hurting in the process is ourselves. Holding on to the hurt, anger, and resentment over time can be harmful to our health and well-being.

> *The only way to win with a toxic person is to not play.*
>
> —Unknown

Forgiveness works both ways. It is the action or process of forgiving or being forgiven. Sometimes it's us who need to say those three important words, "I am sorry," and seek forgiveness.

Why do we feel so compelled to hurt others through our words and our actions? Let me set the record straight: It is not a result of genetic programming. It's learned behavior, and as such, we can all do better.

Here are some ways to avoid those clashes that can lead to hurt feelings and the need to seek forgiveness as a consequence.

1. Don't enter the arena. By choosing not to participate, we avoid getting caught up in the scrum. Sometimes no response can be the best response.
2. Practice R-E-S-P-E-C-T: restraint, education, service, perspective, enlightenment, compassion, tolerance. Avoid the compulsion to hurt others through your words and actions by leaving your ego behind.

3. Reverse the polarity. Find ways to convert those negative situations you encounter into something positive, before they become nuclear events.
4. Work on self-improvement. Becoming the best version of yourself is a full-time job. Put your energy to good use by focusing on improving your *inner space.*

Rolling around in the dirt was fun when we were kids, for some of us anyway (I didn't like to get dirty). However, *news flash*, we are grown-ups now. Who wants to hold grudges and go around being pissed off at the world all the time? Not me. It's high time we start acting like adults. The above is a good place to start.

None of us has led a perfect life. We all make mistakes—mistakes that require forgiveness. When we acknowledge and accept this fact, I believe it becomes easier for us to forgive others.

> *Those who cannot forgive others break the bridge over which they themselves must pass.*
>
> —Confucius

Think about it. Forgiveness is essential to our spiritual growth. If we can't forgive others, how can we expect God to forgive us when the time comes? Forgiveness provides a pathway to healing in body, mind, and spirit. It allows us to let it go and to move forward without continuing to hold on to negative feelings that may have held us back in the past.

It's important to remember that forgiveness is necessary for *our* growth and happiness, not the other party. *Forgiveness* doesn't mean forgetting or excusing the harm done to you or making up with the person who hurt you.

What are the benefits of forgiving someone?

Letting go of grudges and bitterness can make way for improved health and peace of mind. According to the Mayo Clinic Staff, forgiveness can lead to:

- healthier relationships
- improved mental health
- less anxiety, stress, and hostility
- lower blood pressure
- fewer symptoms of depression
- stronger immune system
- improved heart health
- improved self-esteem

Just to be clear: When we forgive, we are not letting the other party off the hook. By letting it go, we're making a conscience decision to not allow those negative feelings we harbor toward the other person to *infect* our lives any longer.

What if I'm unable to let it go?

Ask yourself why. If you're just not ready, you can always set an intention to forgive the person at a later date. Then revisit the issue when you are ready. Don't see yourself ever getting to the point where forgiveness is an option? Then you should seek professional advice to help you work through it.

Keeping the anger and resentment bottled up inside is not healthy and can only manifest itself in more self-destructive ways if left unchecked. Likewise, by holding on to a grudge, you are allowing the other person to have power over you.

Fun fact: *Pistanthrophobia* is the fear of trusting people due to past experiences with relationships gone wrong.

Most people find it easier to forgive a stranger or casual acquaintance than to forgive a loved one. Why is that? Because we have little to nothing *invested* in the relationship with a stranger. With family members, on the other hand, it's different. Family is blood; they mean everything to us.

So when we're hurt by a family member, it cuts us to the core and the hurt is magnified. It is also very personal. Because of this, grudges with family members can go unresolved for decades, and sadly, the love we felt for that person can easily turn to hate over time if the issue is allowed to fester.

In chapter 3 we addressed the fact that in the end, love and relationships are all that truly matter. All relationships, big and small, good and bad, are necessary for our growth and development. Through those people, interactions, and experiences, we learn how to deal with our differences the right way in order to avoid damaging confrontations.

If you have hurt someone by your words and/or actions, then, by all means, work it out. Don't allow it to go on unresolved until it becomes a nuclear event and the relationship cannot be repaired.

1. Fall on the sword—not literally, figuratively.
2. Acknowledge the fact that you made a mistake.
3. Apologize and ask for their forgiveness.
4. Let the person know how much you value the relationship.
5. Allow the other person equal air time to talk it out.
6. Make sure the issue is resolved, so it doesn't resurface.

By taking responsibility (for your part), you are helping to bring closure and allowing the necessary healing to begin. This will enable you, and the other person, to move forward without carrying the baggage of the past discord with you.

Some other important things to remember: Never go to bed angry. The last three words spoken to our loved ones each night should be, "I love you," not, "I am sorry." In all relationships (repeat after me), "If it sounds like crap, don't put it in your mouth!" Hurtful words spoken out of anger will only come back to bite you in the ass later on.

Don't forget to forgive yourself too, when and where needed. Self-forgiveness is very often the first step toward establishing more positive, loving relationships with others. Avoid judging yourself too harshly, which is a tendency we all have. Shut down the negative self-talk ("Stop it!" from chapter 11) that too often invades our inner space.

How do I find it in my heart to forgive those who have hurt me?

"Move on to the next act." As Dr. Wayne Dyer points out, "Your past history and all of your hurts are no longer here in your physical reality. Don't allow them to be here in your mind, muddying your present moments. Your life is like a play with several acts. Some of the characters who enter have short roles to play, others, much larger. Some are villains and others are good guys. But all of them are necessary, otherwise they wouldn't be in the play. Embrace them all, and move on to the next act."

Fun fact: People say "bless you" when you sneeze because your heart stops for a millisecond.

We will all experience hurt, anger, disappointment, and regret in our lifetimes. How we choose to deal with those feelings will help determine our level of happiness and success. The key is to not allow negative situations to gain control of our thoughts and actions. Remember, we can choose to be bitter, or we can choose to get better.

If you are carrying around any of those feelings of anger, disappointment, and resentment today, I would encourage you to let it go. Let go of those past hurts and disappointments, so you can take full advantage of the bright future ahead. This will go a long way to reduce the stress, conflict, and the negativity in your life that oftentimes requires us to seek forgiveness.

Take back your power and learn how to give and to ask for forgiveness. Regardless of our differences, we have at least one thing in common. We're all part of the human race. With this in mind, let's commit to being *more human* and treating each other with *dignity*, *kindness*, and *respect*.

CHAPTER 14
Leadership

If you're not the lead dog on the sled,
the scenery never changes.

In business, market leadership is an essential component for delivering best-in-class profits and shareholder value to the company. However, leadership in today's increasingly global society is less about who is leading the pack and more about how we as individuals can make a difference.

How do we define leadership?

In one respect, leadership is like pornography: it is hard to define, but you know it when you see it. A *leader* is viewed as someone who is in charge or in command of others, while *leadership* has been described as a process of social influence in which one person can enlist the aid and support of others in the accomplishment of a common task. By this definition, each of us has the capacity for leadership through our actions and good deeds.

I have read numerous books and articles on leadership over the years, all trying to get at the essence of leadership, and each have merit. However, my definition is more directed and can be summed up in a concise statement: leadership is making a difference by serving others. You don't have to be a leader to make a difference, but you do need to serve others.

No matter how we choose to define it, leadership in its purest form should be about bringing people together to make something extraordinary happen.

Why is leadership so important?

If you have read my book *Globalization: America's Leadership Challenge Ahead*, you know the answer. Next to spirituality, I believe the thing that is the highest priority, and most sorely lacking, in this country and elsewhere today is *leadership*.

The greatest challenge we face is not the economy. It's not the environment or global warming. It's not poverty, homelessness, world hunger, population growth, scarcity of resources, or lack of world peace. It is a shortage of leadership. There is just not enough high-character leadership to go around to solve all of the problems we face as a global society.

Moreover, at no time in recent history has our faith in leadership in general been tested more. Recent polls reflect the growing dissatisfaction with our leadership in Washington, DC, and this same sentiment carries over to numerous areas of the private sector as well.

Who owns the leadership problem?

The short answer is: we all do. Leadership is not someone else's calling—it is ours as individuals and as members of this global society. Think about it for a moment. Each of us already wears many leadership hats within our families, businesses, communities, churches, and support groups. Developing the necessary confidence in our ability to lead and the capacity for leadership should not be a leap of faith.

"Leadership in difficult times" have unfortunately become the watchwords within our modern society. There is far too much negativity surrounding us, and it's becoming increasingly difficult for positive leadership to rise above it. As Dudley Hall so aptly puts it, "We live in a toxic society where religion and faith have been marginalized, marriage and family trivialized and the free market system demonized."

Our world is more divided than it has been at any point in our lifetimes. However, the challenges we face today are not new ones. Crime and violence, police brutality, political acrimony, wars and conflicts, and terrorism and bad behavior have been with us since the dawn of time. So is leadership in these difficult times any more daunting than the past? Probably not.

However, continuing to operate like we have been will not move us forward. We need major changes in our leadership approach and how we work together. A perfect place to start is within our families and our communities. The next time your child acts out, let them know what they are doing is wrong and correct the behavior. Don't just ignore the issue and think they will grow out of it or throw money at the problem.

When you see someone in harm's way, lend a helping hand. Avoid the temptation to whip out the smartphone camera or look for someone else to come to the rescue. Set a good example by getting involved. Making the hard choices and putting yourself out there is what makes leadership less daunting and more rewarding.

> *You have enemies? Good. That means you've stood for something, sometime in your life.*
>
> —Winston Churchill

What does modern day leadership look like? Just look in the mirror … It begins with you. Leadership opportunities are all around us in the things that we do every day to make a difference for someone else.

- as a parent for a child
- as a teacher for a student
- as a business owner for customers
- as a politician for constituents
- as a pastor for a church member
- as a coach for a player
- as a homeowner for a neighbor
- as a policeman for a stranded motorist
- as a soldier for God and country

This expanded definition of leadership places a much greater emphasis on the influence each one of us has in creating a pathway for people to contribute and to make something extraordinary happen.

We look to those in leadership positions to set the tone by providing focus and clarity, vision, goals and direction, and motivation, as well as to be the catalysts for change. Unfortunately, too many of today's leaders don't measure up to our expectations because we tend to hold them to a higher standard than we do ourselves, and this goes to the root of the problem.

Although the figures aren't available support to this, it's likely that more money has been spent on leadership development during the past three decades in both the public and private sectors than was spent in the previous ten decades combined. So why aren't we turning out better leaders across the board?

There are several factors that could account for this:

1. As I mentioned earlier, leaders are held to a higher standard, and the expectations of leadership today are greater than they have been in the past.
2. The complexity and the rapidity of change that leaders must confront has drastically increased, and as a result, most leaders are ill-prepared to manage this on their own.
3. Virtual real-time access to information through the various media sources and the internet, smartphone cameras, etc. have placed our leaders' public and

private lives under the constant scrutiny of the general public.

4. Our society seeks instant gratification to problem-solving, and this creates unrealistic expectations of our leaders in their efforts to provide short-term solutions to long-term problems.

According to a survey conducted by the Harvard Kennedy School, 68 percent of Americans believe there is a leadership crisis in our country, and leaders in only four of thirteen sectors inspire above-average confidence (the military, the Supreme Court, nonprofits, and medical institutions). It's probably no surprise that leaders in the news media, Congress, and Wall Street received the lowest scores.

How do we restore trust in leadership?

The short answer is: by being positive role models and setting the example. Each of us must assume a broader leadership role within our families, local communities, churches, and workplaces. To restore trust, we must put our differences aside and work *together* to solve the most pressing problems we face locally, nationally, and globally.

Growing up, my generation was blessed with iconic leaders in all areas from government and politics to sports and religion. There were numerous examples of role model leaders, including Dwight D. Eisenhower, John F. and Robert Kennedy, Martin Luther King Jr., Ronald Reagan, Vince Lombardi, John Wooden, and many others. We need more of these role model leaders today in all walks of life.

How can you assume a broader leadership role and become a trusted and effective leader? Start by asking yourself these simple questions at the end of each day:

1. Did I make a real difference today?
2. Did I meet *all* of my commitments?
3. Did I give my best effort to support others?

As a first step, it really doesn't have to be any more complicated than that, despite the challenges ahead of us. Remember too, great leaders come in all sizes, shapes, colors, and faiths. We need role model leaders from all walks of life and all age groups who are committed to solving real-world problems and shaping our future.

Who's driving the bus in your life right now? Is it God, the government, your boss, a family member, or you? When you make a serious commitment to assume broader leadership responsibilities for the actions and the outcomes that affect you, it will make a difference not only in the quality of your life but in the lives of many others.

Professionally or personally, we can't solve all of the world's problems as individuals. However, by working together, we can avoid the train wreck and accomplish great things. So do yourself and others a favor and don't be an observer.

If you want the scenery to change, then put down your smartphone and get off social media. Find a great cause you're passionate about and then work in concert with others to make something extraordinary happen.

CHAPTER 15

The End?

If you are done changing, you're done!

This is the final chapter of the book, but it's not "The End," is it? It's not the end until you stop doing, stop caring, and stop breathing. You're still with me, right?

Good, let's wrap things up because you have a lot of living and a lot of your story that is yet to be written. When we stop to consider the end of our journey here on earth, two questions always seem to surface: "What do I want my legacy to be?" and "Did I make a difference?" Only you can provide answers to these two questions for your life.

If you were granted one more day, what value would you place on it?

Back in 2008, Stanford economists demonstrated that the average value of a year of quality human life is about $129,000 versus $50,000 for the insurance industry. Just take this figure and multiple it by the average life span in years, and there you have it—the value of a human life. The calculation seems to be fairly straightforward, doesn't it?

Today, multiple government agencies have determined the value of a human life to be somewhere between $6 million and $9.1 million. However, real life doesn't work that way, and the answer to the value of one more day would certainly vary for each individual and his or her particular situation. What I can tell you with a high degree of certainty is the value of one more day increases the closer we get to the finish line.

The day my loving wife, Laura, was wheeled into the ICU and we were told she had only two weeks to live, everything changed in an instant. The bucket list of things we had planned to do together in our golden years was now off the table. The remaining time we had together was reduced from years to weeks, days, hours, and minutes. And each of those remaining days we were able to spend with her were *priceless*!

> *When you realize the value of all life, you dwell less on what is past and concentrate more on the preservation of the future.*
>
> —Dian Fossey

Recognize that real life is like a jukebox … and you want the music play on. (For you youngsters, a jukebox is a partially automated music device that plays these ancient vinyl discs we old-timers refer to as *records*.) Sadly, though, far too often we don't hear the music or it's just background noise because we're so busy being busy with our daily routines.

It is not until we are shaken into consciousness by one of those defining moments (birth, death, illness, marriage, divorce, job change or loss, buying or selling a home, relocating, etc.) that we tune into life and pay attention to what is going on in the world around us. It's only then that we hear the music loud and clear. Sound familiar?

Fun fact: You once held a world record when you were born for being the youngest person on the planet. How cool is that?

Sure we all live busy lives, and life can be messy at times, which is why we find it necessary to escape and tune out so often. But what is the alternative? While you consider your response for a moment, recognize that there are four primary phases to all aspects of life in general terms:

- starting
- growing
- repairing
- exiting

The key in each of these areas is to learn and grow from those collective experiences in order to become a better version of you. Get to the really good stuff by peeling away the layers through the self-discovery and growth process. I have tried to build upon each of these various phases through the chapter topics I selected for this book.

We have all had to face adversity. Life is hard and it's not fair, but we can't let setbacks define us. I don't know about you, but I'm out of excuses at this point. Things don't always work out the way we planned, but we have to accept this reality. Looking back, we all have things we would have done differently if we had the opportunity to go back in time.

> *To succeed it's necessary to accept the world as it is and rise above it.*
>
> —Michael Korda

Is there a magic formula for success in navigating through what I refer to as the dark water with the leeches and the snakes? No. There is no magic formula; there is only life and getting the most out of each day. However, here are a few ideas you may want to consider to help you rise above some of the major challenges and avoid being bitten in the ass along the way.

1. Not only expect but prepare for the unexpected. That means anticipating the worst and planning for the best possible outcome in every situation.
2. Stay alert to life's changes and embrace them. Find ways to make each new experience, good or bad, a learning and growth opportunity.
3. Focus on people and not things. Make spending time with the special people in your life each and every day a priority.

4. Never underestimate your impact on the world around you. Don't neglect the opportunity to assist someone in finding his or her own music.

Back to the original question: if you were granted one more day, what value would you place on it? The answer is immaterial. Why? Because its value changes with each passing day until it becomes a priceless commodity at the end.

Every new day we are granted is an amazing gift, and it's up to us to make it count. As I have stated in previous chapters, each of us has the capacity to change and grow and will accomplish great things in our lifetimes. What is most important is how we use the time available to us and the impact we have on the people around us.

Fun fact: Jellyfish and lobsters are considered biologically immortal. They don't age and will never die unless they are killed.

Now, here are some valuable life lessons to take with you that my son, Daniel, and I took away from our holiday cooking adventure a few years back. These lessons apply to so many different areas of life that I did not want to close out the final chapter without sharing them with you.

1. Teamwork and communication are keys to success in any endeavor.
2. Don't expect perfection. Even when you follow the script perfectly, success is not guaranteed.

3. Failure is not final. It's okay to start over if you miss the mark the first time.
4. Great results require skillful preparation, planning, hard work, and luck.
5. Get help, advice, and wise counsel from the experts when you're stuck.
6. Timing is everything! If you spend too much time doing anything, it will result in burnout.
7. Mistakes or missteps can sometimes produce some wonderful surprises.
8. Keep life simple. It's less work and stress on everyone's part.
9. Take time out to celebrate your accomplishments, both large and small.
10. Don't take other people and their contributions for granted.

To put the value of life in perspective, I thoroughly enjoyed Joel Osteen's March 26 message in *Your Best Life Begins Each Morning*. "A beat up hundred-dollar bill is still worth a hundred dollars."

That's the way God sees each of us, and it's how we should view ourselves. We will all go through challenges and struggles. But, in fact, we will never, ever lose our value.

How will you use the time you've been granted to make a difference and improve the quality of life?

When we recognize that all life is precious, we take extra care in preserving it. Use the time you have left wisely to make the world a better and safer place for all. Keep on changing, growing, creating, and helping others through your experiences.

There are only two certainties in life: death and taxes. As we grow older, the thoughts of our mortality become more evident. Questions about our legacy, too, become more a part of our thoughts. The thing each of us has in common is the desire to make a difference—to know our lives had purpose and meaning.

If you were to describe your legacy in ten words today, what words would you choose? I know, that's really deep stuff. As my daughter, Melanie, would say, "Dad, you're having one of those Zen moments," and she would probably be right. However, just think about that for a few moments and then write down those ten words, so you can refer back to them periodically to see how they evolve over time.

Whether you realize it or not, your legacy is every life you touch. As you are writing the remaining chapters of your life's story (and that happy ending), make sure the pages are filled with wonderful memories and those great life experiences shared with others.

This is not the end. Stay positive about your life, the possibilities for a bright future, and the road ahead. May your life's story be an inspiration to others and a story you will be proud to tell your children and grandchildren someday.

ABOUT THE AUTHOR

John Carroll is the founder and CEO of Tres Coaching Services™, a business and leadership coaching, consulting, and training services practice. He is a visionary, results-driven business leader known for his keen ability to drive transformation and change, and deliver outstanding results in highly competitive start-up, turnaround and high growth markets.

During his distinguished 30-year corporate career, John held executive positions in Fortune 1000, midsize, and emerging companies, leading high-performing business divisions that generated more than $1 billion in sales. Since 2003, he has successfully launched three companies and has worked with hundreds of business leaders to improve the growth, profitability and performance of their businesses through his Professional Coaching, Business Leaders Forum[SM] mastermind programs, and his online course 'Discover YOUR Formula for Success'.

Mr. Carroll is the author of *Globalization: America's Leadership Challenge Ahead*, the coauthor of Amazon best-seller, *Power of Inspiration: Dare to Be the Best You!*, and the contributing author for *The Life of a Gentleman.* He's also a highly regarded blogger and speaker, and has been recognized by both Who's Who in Executives and Professionals and the Global Registry of Outstanding Professionals and Entrepreneurs for his sales and leadership achievements.

John has three adult children and three grandchildren and resides in Keller, Texas. For more information, visit trescoach.com or contact John via email at john@trescoach.com.

BIBLIOGRAPHY

Bell, Alisa. *50 Golden Nuggets: Laser Sharp Quotes Designed to Shape Your Day.* Bloomington, IN: AuthorHouse, 2016.

Buford, Bob. *Halftime: Moving from Success to Significance.* Grand Rapids, MI: Zondervan, 1994.

Carroll, John. *Globalization: America's Leadership Challenge Ahead.* Keller, TX: TresCoach Books, 2011-12.

Covey, Stephen. *The 7 Habits of Highly Effective People.* New York: Simon & Schuster, 1989, 2004.

Dunn, Lauren. "Be thankful: Science says gratitude is good for your health". TODAY, 26 Nov 2015.

Dyer, Dr. Wayne W. "How To Forgive Someone Who Has Hurt You: In 15 Steps". Wayne's Blog – DrWayneDyer.com.

Emmons, Robert A. "Gratitude is good medicine". UC Davis Medical Center, 25 Nov 2015.

Feldman, Robert S. "UMass Amherst Researcher Finds Most People Lie in Everyday Conversation". UMass Amherst News & Media Relations, 10 Jun 2012.

Gladwell, Malcolm. *Outliers: The Story of Success.* New York: Little, Brown and Company, 2008.

Hoomans, Dr. Joel. "35,000 Decisions: The Great Choices of Strategic Leaders". Leading Edge Journal, 20 Mar 2015.

Kingsbury, Kathleen. "The Value of a Human Life: $129,000". Time, 20 May 2008.

Leonard, George. *Mastery: The Keys to Success and Long-Term Fulfillment.* New York: A Plume Book, 1992.

Midgley, Lauren. *It's 6 a.m. and I'm Already Behind: 30 Strategies to Get Caught Up in a Crazy-Busy World.* Colleyville, TX: Focused Action Publishing, 2015.

Osteen, Joel. *Your Best Life Begins Each Morning: Devotions to Start Every Day of the Year.* New York: Hachette Book Group USA, 2008.

Pink, Daniel. *Drive: The Surprising Truth About What Motivates Us.* New York: Burkhead Books, 2009.

Rosenthal, S. A. *National Leadership Index 2012: A National Study of Confidence in Leadership.* Center for Public Leadership, Harvard Kennedy School, Harvard University, 2012.

Segran, Elizabeth. "When Lying Is Good". Fast Company, 17 Sep 2014.

St. John, Richard. "Success is a continuous journey". TED Talk – TED.com, 15 Feb 2009.

Taylor, Jim, Ph.D. "Personal Growth: Motivation: The Drive to Change". Psychology Today, 02 Jan 2012.

Thaik, Cynthia M., M.D. "Self-Doubt: Junk Food for the Heart". Psychology Today, 07 May 2013.

United Nations Department of Economic and Social Affairs. "The World Population Prospects: 2015 Revision". New York, 29 Jul 2015.

Various Authors. *Power of Inspiration: Dare to Be the Best YOU!*. North Richland Hills, TX: Light Point Press, 2013.

Warren, Rick. *The Purpose Driven Life: What on Earth Am I Here For?*. Grand Rapids, MI: Zondervan, 2002, 2011, 2012.

Wong, Brittany. "10 Relationship Facts Everyone Should Know Before Getting Married". Huff Post US, 27 Mar 2017.

Ziglar, Zig. "Zig Ziglar Cooked In The Squat". Online video clip. YouTube. Inspire Motivate, 15 Jun 2010.

Printed in the United States
By Bookmasters